Mercedes-Benz 300SL

MERCEDES-BENZ 300SL

Dennis Adler

Motorbooks International
Publishers & Wholesalers

To Jeanne,
For always being there

First published in 1994 by Motorbooks International Publishers & Wholesalers, PO Box 2, 729 Prospect Avenue, Osceola, WI 54020 USA

© Dennis Adler 1994

Motorbooks International books are also available at discounts in bulk quantity for industrial or sales-promotional use. For details write to Special Sales Manager at the Publisher's address

Library of Congress Cataloging-in-Publication Data Available

ISBN 0-87938-882-X

On the front cover: Mercedes-Benz 300SL roadster owned by Dr. Barry Gruer and 300SL coupe owned by Claus Meese.

On the frontispiece: A 300SL coupe seen from above with Gullwing doors open. The most rare color among 300SLs, Strawberry Red was only applied to thirteen coupes.

On the title pages: An aluminum-alloy-bodied 300SL coupe at speed. One of the rarest 300SL models, only twenty-nine alloy-bodied coupes were produced. This is the very first car built, body number 5500001, chassis number 5500173.

On the back cover: The 300SL line from the early Gullwing coupes (silver car) to the later Gullwings (red coupe) through two versions of the 300SL roadster, the latter fitted with a removable hardtop (black car) and listed as a roadster coupe.

Printed and bound in Hong Kong

CONTENTS

	PREFACE	7
CHAPTER 1	**THOSE MAGNIFICENT CARS FROM STUTTGART**	11
	300SL COUPE AND ROADSTER	
CHAPTER 2	**RUDOLF UHLENHAUT: THE MAN BEHIND THE STAR**	19
	THE STORY BEGINS....	
CHAPTER 3	**FROM RACE CARS TO ROAD CAR**	33
	TO NEW YORK CITY VIA THE NÜRBURGRING	
CHAPTER 4	**THE 300SL COUPE**	63
	ON ROAD AND TRACK	
CHAPTER 5	**THE 300SL ROADSTER**	97
	FROM WINGS TO WIND	
CHAPTER 6	**THE 300SLR**	129
	THE FORMULA FOR RACING	
CHAPTER 7	**THE RESTORERS**	147
	REVERSING THE AGING PROCESS	
APPENDICES	**DESIGN CHANGES AND OPTIONS**	162
	SPECIFICATIONS	164
	PRODUCTION HISTORY	166
	INDEX	168

PREFACE

As an automotive historian, I often find myself presented opportunities few people ever experience. Over the years I have been privileged to ride along with racing legends Jackie Stewart, Dan Gurney, Phil Hill and Bob Bondurant. I have also had the chance to chat with many of the world's greatest automotive designers, including Gordon Buehrig, Franklin Q. Hershey, Ralph Roberts, Sergio Pininfarina, Carroll Shelby, and many others. And there have been occasions when car owners were gracious enough to toss me the keys to their vehicles; I have had the occasion to drive a Bugatti Royale, a Ferrari 250 GTO, countless Porsches, and one of my all-time favorites, the Mercedes-Benz 300SL.

My first experience with this car was in the late 1970s when photographing a 300SL roadster for *Car Classics* magazine. The owner said that I should drive the car for the afternoon. "That was the only way to truly appreciate it," he told me. Indeed it was. From the moment I first cranked the engine to life, I have had the highest regard for these remarkable cars. To my way of thinking, the 300SL, along with the E-Type Jaguars, share the honor of being the most romantic motorcars of the postwar era.

The name Mercedes-Benz was so profoundly rooted in automotive history that in many respects Mercedes-Benz *is* automotive history. Whatever emotional lines may have been drawn by wars and politics over the years, the cars have somehow managed to rise above them.

I cannot imagine what that great legend-maker Max Hoffman must have thought the first time he laid eyes on a 300SL. Surely he knew that this car would be warmly received by his customers in the United States just as he had known the 356 Porsche and so many other European marques would be met with glee and open garages by automotive enthusiasts and connoisseurs from coast to coast. Yet unlike the 356, the 300SL was a car destined only for the elite—industrialists, entrepreneurs, actors, entertainers, and America's cafe society. The 300SL was priced beyond the reach of average men from the beginning, and it remains so to this day.

No, I didn't get all this from my first drive in a 300SL. I was merely thrilled with the car's performance and style. Years later, I had

Mercedes-Benz 300SL roadster owned by Dr. Barry Gruer and 300SL coupe owned by Claus Meese

the opportunity to drive J. B. Nethercutt's coupe for an entire day. Afterwards I made it a point to get behind the wheel of an SL whenever the chance presented itself. And after perhaps a dozen times over the years and as many articles, I have come to appreciate these cars for what they were, and even more so, for what they are: An extraordinary example of masterful engineering and beguiling design in perfect harmony. An amalgam every automobile manufacturer seeks and so few achieve.

It has been forty years since the 300SL coupe was introduced at the 1954 New York International Motor Sports Show. Since then, these cars have been driven into history, raced, wrecked, restored, shown at concours d'elegance, and elevated by collectors to a plane on level with fine art.

All of this veneration over a mixture of light alloys, steel, copper, glass, wool, and gaberdine? It would appear that the men of Mercedes-Benz had such a goal in mind when they created the 300SL. But in truth, the only serious objective they had was to build the best car they could. That they did. The rest is what we have made of it.

The creation of almost anything worthwhile takes time and great effort, and particularly the creation of a book covering the history of so popular and highly regarded an automobile as the 300SL.

No book of this magnitude could be written without following in the footsteps of the many accomplished authors and historians who have preceded me down this road. Many books were examined in compiling this one, most notably the limited Art & Color Edition of German author Jürgen Lewandowski's *Mercedes-Benz 300 SL*, of which only 3,000 copies were printed. This stands in my mind as one of the finest examples in the world of quality European book publishing. Another is Richard M. Langworth's *Mercedes-Benz: The First Hundred Years* (Publications International, 1984), itself a brilliant compendium of works including excerpts from Karl Ludvigsen's now out-of-print history *The Mercedes-Benz Racing Cars* (Bond-Parkhurst, 1971), and Alfred Neubauer's memoirs, *Speed Was My Life* (Clarkson Potter, 1960).

A book that has become an invaluable source for historical reference over the years is Werner Oswald's *Mercedes-Benz Personenwagen 1886-1984* (Motorbuch Verlag, Stuttgart, 1985), of which my only regret is that its entire text is in German! Other valuable references have been those of Mercedes-Benz Club of America associate W. Robert Nitske, whose in-depth research at the Daimler-Benz Museum in Stuttgart, brought light to many questions about the 300SL in two fine volumes, *The Mercedes-Benz 300SL* (Motorbooks International, 1974), and *Mercedes-Benz: A History* (Motorbooks International, 1975). In addition, the fine Mercedes-Benz publication *The Star And The Laurel* by Beverly Rae Kimes, (Mercedes-Benz North America, 1986), *Mercedes-Benz 300 SL Gull-Wing & Roadster* by William Boddy (Osprey Publishing Limited, London, and Motorbooks International, 1983), and *Mercedes-Benz Design* by Bruno Sacco, Director of Design for Daimler-Benz AG, (Mercedes-Benz North America, 1988), all provided valuable information for my research.

There are the many individuals who have also contributed to this effort, including A. B. Shuman, Fred Heiler, and Lois Anderson of Mercedes-Benz North America, who allowed me to utilize the corporate historical archives in my research; T. C. Browne, for his valuable assistance; my friend and associate Frank Barrett, publisher and editor of *The Star*, the official publication of the Mercedes-Benz Club of

America; automotive restorers Scott Grundfor and Jerry Hjeltness; and John Olson, editor of the *SL Marketletter*.

The author would like to extend his thanks to the Gull Wing Group, Inc., Jerry and Eric Hjeltness of Hjeltness Restorations Inc., Escondido, California, and the owners of the 300SLs featured in this book for their extraordinary cooperation and assistance in the creation of this book: Jerry and Eric Hjeltness, John Moore (strawberry coupe); Ernst Wiles (strawberry roadster); Pat Smiekel (red Gullwing, silver gray Gullwing, black roadster coupe, and red roadster); Claus Meese (burgundy coupe); and Dr. Barry Gruer (ivory roadster). Additional thanks to Stephan Cobos and the staff of Scott Restorations, Scott Grundfor, and Santiago Maspons (silver and plaid coupe). Thanks as well to Pat Smiekel (Porsche 356 Speedster) and Ron Pinto (Ferrari 212 Inter).

Without the help of these experts, and that of the generous owners who provided the cars for my photography, this book would not have been possible.

My profound thanks to one and all.

Dennis A. Adler
Pennsylvania
February 1994

THOSE MAGNIFICENT CARS FROM STUTTGART

300SL COUPE AND ROADSTER

During an era when automobile styling had become almost hidebound throughout Europe, Mercedes-Benz so outpaced its contemporaries with the 300SL that its design and engineering standards became the hallmark by which sports cars the world over would be judged for more than a decade.

No other postwar models of German, British, or Italian origin could equal the engineering, precision, and quality of the 300SL, a single master stroke so sweeping as to be without precedent. You could have almost made a similar claim regarding Porsche, Ferrari, or Jaguar in the 1950s, but each at its best was less than the sum of the 300SL. Ferrari had its magnificent V-12 engines, Porsche its innovative engineering, and the Jaguar XK-120 its dashing good looks. But none could claim the same synergy of chassis, suspension, and engine design, combined with a purity of styling and quality of construction, that Daimler-Benz offered. The aggressive styling of Italian and British sports cars, however appealing, looked almost antiquated alongside the dramatic shape of the 300SL.

That offspring of racing, the 300SL coupe, went into limited production in 1954 as a luxurious adaptation of the triumphant 1952 Mercedes-Benz competition cars. Perhaps it was that perceptible affiliation between race car and road car that made the production models such enduring favorites. In the single year in which Daimler-Benz AG campaigned the 300SL, they finished first and second in all but its maiden race, the grueling Mille Miglia, where one 300SL finished second—just 4 minutes behind Giovanni Bracco's winning Ferrari 250MM—and another fourth, with drivers Karl Kling and the legendary Rudolf Caracciola. After Italy, the factory team never again saw the exhaust of another car across the finish line. Mercedes-Benz finished first, second, and third at the Grand Prix of Berne, where Caracciola crashed, never to race again. The team was first and second in the 1952 24 Heures du Mans, and at the Nürburgring, 300SLs crossed the finish line first through fourth, with the debut of the car in roadster form. Virtually unbeatable wherever they ran, the factory cars wound up their racing career with a hard-fought one-two finish in the

The 300SL line from the early Gullwing coupes (silver car) to the later Gullwings (red coupe) through two versions of the 300SL roadster, the latter fitted with a removable hardtop (black car) and listed as a roadster coupe.

1952 Carrera PanAmericana.

For one season, Mercedes-Benz literally dominated European sports car racing, and having demonstrated once again that Daimler-Benz quality, engineering, and reliability were supreme, the 300SLs were withdrawn from competition. There had been faster cars at every race, but none better built; the 300SLs either outran or outlasted the Ferraris, Jaguars—*alles*.

The unprecedented success of the 300SL captured the attention of automakers and auto enthusiasts the world over. It also caught the eye of Austro-American importer and automotive entrepreneur Max Hoffman. Hoffman wasn't necessarily a visionary, but

he was a businessman with *vision*, a keen sense for what would sell to American automotive enthusiasts. With an elegant Frank Lloyd Wright-designed showroom at 1739 Broadway in New York City, Hoffman was involved in bringing Porsche, BMW, Jaguar, Alfa Romeo, and Mercedes-Benz to the United States when these makes were virtually unknown.

The production version of the 300SL captured the look, and to a great extent, the performance of the race cars but embellished it with the hand-crafted luxury for which Daimler-Benz had become renowned.

The racing engine and lightweight body had to be altered considerably to meet production-car requirements, yet the fraternal relationship between the cars that had swept the 1952 season and those that would sweep sports car enthusiasts off their feet throughout the 1950s was unmistakable.

The most notable mechanical difference between the 1952 competition cars and the 1954 production coupes was the fuel delivery system. The competition cars had used three Solex 40 PBJC downdraft carburetors and twin electric fuel pumps; the 3.0 liter engines for the 1954 models received fuel through direct mechanical injection, the only such application of this system in a series-production, gasoline-powered automobile.

Based on its experience with diesel power, Daimler-Benz and Bosch had pioneered direct fuel injection in the 1930s for aircraft engine applications. Daimler-Benz had also experimented with a fuel-injected 4.5 liter V-12 racing engine in 1939 and at one point had considered using direct fuel injection for the 1952 competition cars.

The 300SL engine, was a direct adaptation of the single-overhead-cam, six-cylinder

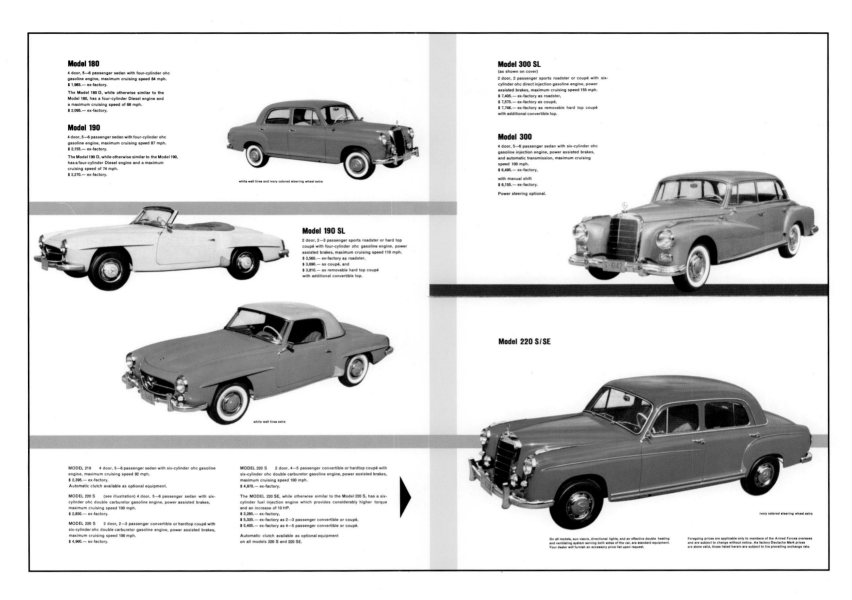

Model 180

4 door, 5—6 passenger sedan with four-cylinder ohc gasoline engine, maximum cruising speed 84 mph.
$ 1,985.— ex-factory.

The Model 180 D, while otherwise similar to the Model 180, has a four-cylinder Diesel engine and a maximum cruising speed of 68 mph.
$ 2,095.— ex-factory.

Model 190

4 door, 5—6 passenger sedan with four-cylinder ohc gasoline engine, maximum cruising speed 87 mph.
$ 2,155.— ex-factory.

The Model 190 D, while otherwise similar to the Model 190, has a four-cylinder Diesel engine and a maximum cruising speed of 74 mph.
$ 2,270.— ex-factory.

white wall tires and ivory colored steering wheel extra

Model 190 SL

2 door, 2—3 passenger sports roadster or hard top coupé with four-cylinder ohc gasoline engine, power assisted brakes, maximum cruising speed 110 mph.
$ 3,560.— ex-factory as roadster,
$ 3,690.— as coupé, and
$ 3,810.— as removable hard top coupé with additional convertible top.

white wall tires extra

MODEL 219   4 door, 5—6 passenger sedan with six-cylinder ohc gasoline engine, maximum cruising speed 92 mph.
$ 2,395.— ex-factory.
Automatic clutch available as optional equipment.

MODEL 220 S   (see illustration) 4 door, 5—6 passenger sedan with six-cylinder ohc double carburetor gasoline engine, power assisted brakes, maximum cruising speed 100 mph.
$ 2,850.— ex-factory.

MODEL 220 S   2 door, 2—3 passenger convertible or hardtop coupé with six-cylinder ohc double carburetor gasoline engine, power assisted brakes, maximum cruising speed 100 mph.
$ 4,900.— ex-factory.

MODEL 220 S   2 door, 4—5 passenger convertible or hardtop coupé with six-cylinder ohc double carburetor gasoline engine, power assisted brakes, maximum cruising speed 100 mph.
$ 4,970.— ex-factory.

The MODEL 220 SE, while otherwise similar to the Model 220 S, has a six-cylinder fuel injection engine which provides considerably higher torque and an increase of 10 HP.
$ 3,285.— ex-factory,
$ 5,335.— ex-factory as 2—3 passenger convertible or coupé,
$ 5,405.— ex factory as 4—5 passenger convertible or coupé.

Automatic clutch available as optional equipment on all models 220 S and 220 SE.

Model 300 SL

(as shown on cover)

2 door, 2 passenger sports roadster or coupé with six-cylinder ohc direct injection gasoline engine, power assisted brakes, maximum cruising speed 155 mph.
$ 7,405.— ex-factory as roadster,
$ 7,575.— ex-factory as coupé,
$ 7,746.— ex-factory as removable hard top coupé with additional convertible top.

Model 300

4 door, 5—6 passenger sedan with six-cylinder ohc gasoline injection engine, power assisted brakes, and automatic transmission, maximum cruising speed 100 mph.
$ 6,495.— ex-factory,

with manual shift
$ 6,155.— ex-factory.

Power steering optional.

Model 220 S/SE

On all models, sun visors, directional lights, and an effective double heating and ventilating system serving both sides of the car, are standard equipment. Your dealer will furnish an accessory price list upon request.

Foregoing prices are applicable only to members of the Armed Forces overseas and are subject to change without notice. As factory Deutsche Mark prices are alone valid, those listed herein are subject to the prevailing exchange rate.

ivory colored steering wheel extra

powerplant used in the 300 Series sedan, coupe, cabriolet, and roadster. The main differences were due to its mounting: the car's low hood line had forced the designers to tilt the engine to the left 50 degrees from the vertical in both the competition cars and the production models, so the 300SL engine had a sloped head face, with combustion chambers extending into pockets in the block. A dry-sump oiling system also helped reduce engine height and provided better oil cooling. To assure reliability, each engine was run-in on the dynamometer for thirty-two hours before it was installed.

The maximum 215bhp arrived at the rear wheels via a four-speed synchromesh gearbox and a ZF limited-slip differential. At peak performance the production 300SL could at-

The Daimler-Benz line for the early 1950s; the 300SL was featured on the brochure's front cover.
Frank Barrett Collection

tain 150mph and reach 60mph from rest in eight seconds. For privateer competition, the cars could be ordered with a 4.11:1 rear-axle ratio (designed for hill climbs or short American road courses) or a choice of either 3.89:1; 3.64:1 (the most common on Gullwings in the United States); 3.42:1 for higher top speeds; or the 3.25:1, which allowed the highest maximum speed. With the 3.25 rear axle the terminal velocity (as tested by Daimler-Benz), was a remarkable 161.5mph. Realistically, the cars could easily reach 150mph, making them the fastest production automobiles available in 1954.

The 300SL, for all its power, was also a forgiving automobile; it could be driven wide open or at a gentle pace with equal ease. One could cruise comfortably at 40mph in top gear and with a firm application of your right foot, be up to more than 130mph in moments. Perhaps the real attraction of this car was not in actually committing such an act, but in knowing that one could. In any case, the mechanical fuel injection played a big part in this flexibility by allowing more precise control of mixture and fuel flow over widely varying conditions.

Another feature adding to the allure of this automobile was the chassis beneath the SL, an intricate cross-braced matrix of thin, straight tubes supporting the body, engine, and independent front and rear suspensions. Similar in design to the spaceframe used in the competition cars, its uppermost tubes surrounded the passenger compartment at about the level of the driver's elbow, and—as in the race cars—doors that opened upward.

The four-wheel, fully independent suspension systems used on both the competition cars and the production coupes, was again based on the Mercedes-Benz 300 Series, using the 300 Sedan's front and two-part rear swing axle design. For the SLs, coil springs and tubular shock absorbers were used at all four wheels, and drum brakes for the coupes utilized the new Al-Fin process, whereby a cast-iron liner was shrunk into a finned aluminum-alloy drum, providing a good friction surface and relatively low weight as well as improved heat dissipation. As it was one of the largest drum brakes ever installed on a production automobile, a vacuum brake booster was added to keep pedal effort reasonable.

A similar size record may have been set by the huge 130 liter fuel tank (roughly 34 gallons), which left little room in the trunk for anything more than the spare tire. The designers made amends by offering an optional set of leather luggage designed to fit snugly (in every sense of the word) on the package shelf behind the seats.

Outside, the vestigial image of a race car remained, while to the driver the 300SL was very much a *boulevardier*, decked out with luxurious trappings: Optional leather upholstery or standard gaberdine plaid and tex-leather, stylish brightwork, superb attention to detail, and well-placed instruments.

The only feature of the 300SL that frustrated even the most avid enthusiast was the means by which driver and passenger entered and, worse, were forced to exit through the Gullwing's upswung portals. The process as explained by German historian Jürgen Lewandowski:

"To enter the car elegantly, you unlock the steering wheel, swivel it to an almost horizontal position and sit down on the doorsill.

The 300SL became a sensation in the United States and importer Max Hoffman had legions of customers from Palm Springs to Palm Beach. The greatest percentage of 300SL coupes built were sold through Hoffman's New York and Los Angeles dealerships.

Straightforward yet graceful: the rear emblem denoting the 300SL designation on a roadster.

The exquisite cockpit of the 300SL roadster brought jet-age styling and controls to the affluent owner.

Now, pull up your legs, lift them over the sill and carefully move them into the footwell. As soon as you feel properly installed, put your right arm on the right side of the bucket seat and push yourself up on the doorsill with your left arm. This will enable you to gracefully slide into the surprisingly comfortable bucket seat, then swivel the steering wheel back into its normal position." This is probably why the 300SL was seldom used by bank robbers as a getaway car....

Another common complaint was the coupe's ventilation system, or lack thereof—limited only to a cowl duct, wind wings, and removable side windows. However, the sheer enjoyment of driving the car more than made up for all of these minor inconveniences.

Total production for the coupe was 1,400 from 1954 to 1957. That number also included a limited run of twenty-nine aluminum-bodied cars built for sports car club competition.

As Daimler-Benz closed the Gullwing's doors for the last time, waiting to take its place was a new 300SL, a sportier, more practical roadster model, introduced at the Geneva Automobile Show in March 1957. If it were possible to imagine, the roadster was even more imposing than the coupe.

The front end of the roadster was modified with a new, more modern headlight configuration, while underneath, the new body was set atop a redesigned tubular frame, providing the added structural integrity required of a convertible body with conventional doors.

In addition to a folding top, and significantly easier entry and exit, the roadster also had an improved rear suspension. The coupe had used a conventional swing axle with two pivot points outboard of the differential. If driven on trailing throttle through a tight curve, the camber change tended to lift the inside rear wheel and induce sudden oversteer. This was great for race drivers, but harsh on those not endowed with the skills of Stirling Moss. Thus, the roadster was fitted with a new swing axle, utilizing a single, low pivot point, which improved the car's corner-ing behavior and predictability. The horizontal compensating spring included with the new axle also gave the roadster a somewhat gentler ride.

Improvements in the engine compartment, including a standard-equipment sports camshaft, provided an additional 20 horsepower to 235bhp in US trim, making it not only a better-handling car than its Gullwing predecessor, but a quicker one too, despite a 200lb weight penalty. With the addition of Dunlop disc brakes in March 1961 and an optional removable hardtop, the roadster reached its highest level of development, the final evolution of the 300SL.

When roadster production ended in 1963, a total of 1,858 had been built over a seven-year period. Not many in the overall scheme of things automotive, but few enough and great enough to warrant their veneration as the most important sports cars of their time, and perhaps all time.

The 300SL coupe and roadster were the products of an era in Mercedes-Benz history that passed in the blinking of an eye—but have yet to fade from sight.

RUDOLF UHLENHAUT:
THE MAN BEHIND THE STAR

THE STORY BEGINS....

Behind every great sports car built in the last half century there has been a guiding hand—a designer, an engineer, or perhaps someone with a dream. You can always find that exceptional individual who took a pencil-drawn sketch and gave it substance and life. Some of these legendary innovators are obvious by name: Enzo Ferrari, the Maserati brothers, and W. O. Bentley. Others are remembered through the machines they created: Sir William Lyons and the magnificent XK-120 and E-Type Jaguars; Colin Chapman and the Lotus; and David Brown for all the great postwar Aston Martins. At Daimler-Benz, many names can be found contributing to the 300SL's genesis— Alfred Neubauer, Fritz Nallinger, Karl Wilfert, even Max Hoffman. But it was Rudolf Uhlenhaut who did the mid-wifery.

Rudolf Uhlenhaut was born July 15, 1906, son of a German bank director and an English mother. He was educated in Great Britain and Germany, earning a degree in mechanical engineering in 1931 from the Munich Technical Institute. Uhlenhaut began his forty-one-year career with

Daimler-Benz that same year as a passenger-car test engineer.

His easy-going manner and reputation for finding creative solutions to engineering problems helped him to advance within five years

Until 1972, Rudolf Uhlenhaut served as Director of Passenger Car Development for Daimler-Benz AG. Near his retirement, he was quoted as saying that, in his view, the most significant factor in the company's comeback after the Second World War was the Mercedes overhead-cam six-cylinder engine. Indeed, it was the foundation upon which so much of his work in the early postwar era was based.
Daimler-Benz AG

Opposite page
The grille of the 300SL wore Daimler-Benz's famous three-pointed star.

to the position of Technical Director in charge of race-car construction and testing. At the time of his appointment in 1936, Daimler-Benz race cars were being trounced so badly that the company had actually withdrawn from several events toward the end of the season. Uhlenhaut was just 30 years old when he was given the assignment of turning this situa-

tion around, which he did in less than a year's time. By 1937, he had returned the Mercedes-Benz "Silver Arrows" to the competition forefront with the W125 Grand Prix car.

In 1937, the W125s won the Tripoli, German, Avus, Eifel, Monaco, Swiss, Italian, and Czech Grands Prix. Uhlenhaut and his team later guaranteed Daimler-Benz dominance of

Grand Prix racing for the rest of the decade with the W154 and W163 GP cars.

It was during this period in his career that Uhlenhaut developed his driving skills to the extent that he could easily have become a champion race driver himself. By 1939, he was as fast as anyone on the Mercedes-Benz team, if not faster, and often would investigate complaints about a race car being down on speed by taking it out himself and carefully analyzing its performance from behind the wheel.

It has been written that he had been soundly admonished by his superiors, not just for test-driving the racing cars, but for doing so at speeds that rivalled the team's aces. By the 1950s Rudolf Uhlenhaut was in a class with World Driving Champion Juan Manuel Fangio. Of course, Uhlenhaut was far too valuable to Daimler-Benz as an engineer and designer to be put at risk in competition. Nevertheless, his abilities behind the wheel allowed him to develop cars not only from an engineer's viewpoint, but from a race driver's as well. A talent with which few designers have been blessed.

Phil Hill, America's first World Driving Champion, knew Uhlenhaut throughout much of his career. "He was held in the highest esteem by drivers, because he was an engineer who could drive.... All those stories about Uhlenhaut being able to drive Mercedes GP cars at competitive speeds around circuits such as the Nürburgring were true, and that's no mean feat," said Hill.

The driving force behind the Daimler-Benz racing team, Alfred Neubauer was a brilliant strategist who guided his team from the pits as though he were behind the wheel of every car.
Daimler-Benz AG

Members of the famous Mercedes-Benz design and racing team following a race: driver Karl Kling, pictured with his wife, Uhlenhaut (holding the Gullwing door), Fritz Nallinger, and to the far right, Alfred Neubauer.
Daimler-Benz AG

Opposite page

As a starting point, the 300
sedan was admittedly a big
car, but it had the engine
size Mercedes needed. The
300SL would utilize as many
components from the sedan
as deemed feasible for racing:
rear axle, transmission,
front and rear suspension.
One advantage of the sedan
was that Mercedes-Benz
already had a workable
four-wheel independent
suspension system.

During the Second World War, Uhlenhaut was assigned to work on arctic-weather vehicles for the German army. He later managed one of the small aircraft engine plants that had been built in the German countryside to escape the heavy Allied bombings that were leveling much of Stuttgart and surrounding industrial areas. For two years after the war, Uhlenhaut worked for an REME (Royal Engineers, Mechanical/Electrical) unit of the British Occupational Army.

Before his return to DBAG, Rudi worked on structural theories with British Army engineers, making tube-frame models and then intentionally breaking them to find ways of inceasing tensile strength while reducing mass. These experiments would later become the foundation for Uhlenhaut's triangulated spaceframe design.

Upon returning to Daimler-Benz in 1948, he was appointed chief of the experimental department. As head of Research and Development, Uhlenhaut was responsible for the factory's postwar racing program, while the legendary Alfred Neubauer resumed di-

Mercedes-Benz 300SL

The 300 sedan was powered by a 2996cc six-cylinder inline power unit with a compression ratio of 6.4:1 and output of 115bhp. Rugged and simple in design, the engine was built for sturdiness and minimum wear. Although it would ultimately enjoy numerous modifications, the final version used in the 300SL relied heavily on the original design.

Opposite page
The fuel-injected production 300SL engine bore little resemblance to the carbureted 300 sedan's inline six, yet the two were very much the same in basic design. Uhlenhaut was able to coax 170hp from the 3.0 liter engine without increasing its displacement.

rection of the works race team in 1951.

Rudolf Uhlenhaut was facing a difficult challenge in his new position, that of repeating what he had done for Daimler-Benz in the late 1930s with the W125. Now, however, he had little more than production-car engines and spare parts at his disposal and the budget allocated by Daimler-Benz for developing competition cars was less than adequate to match Neubauer's vision of a factory racing effort.

Even as late as 1951, Mercedes-Benz was working with fundamentally prewar designs, and its 300 Series flagship models were in many respects the last vestiges of a bygone era, with body lines still reminiscent of the late 1930s. The first truly modern Mercedes-Benz models would not appear until 1954. Thus, the 1952 300SL race cars and the production versions that followed two years later were significant for their advanced exterior styling. In addition, the 190SL roadster ap-

The 300SLR competition

roadsters were driven by

Stirling Moss and Juan

Manuel Fangio in the 1955

Mille Miglia. Moss took the

checkered flag with Fangio

a frustrated second.

peared at the same time as the 300SL coupe in 1954, and this more affordable open air version, sharing a similar body design, was on the market two years before the 300SL appeared in roadster form.

Having watched Jaguar dominate the French twenty-four-hour day-into-night marathon at Le Mans in 1951, Uhlenhaut and his close associate Fritz Nallinger, DBAG's Technical Director, reasoned that they could do essentially

XK Series six; for Daimler-Benz it would be the single-overhead-cam six from the Type 300 and 300S. The competition cars could also utilize other 300S components deemed suitable for competition: rear axle, transmission, and front and rear suspension.

As a starting point, the 300 sedan was admittedly a big, heavy cumbersome car in comparison to a Jaguar XK-120. But it had the engine size Mercedes needed in order to keep up with its rivals' powerful sports cars: a 2996cc six-cylinder inline power unit with a compression ratio of 6.4:1 and an output of 115bhp at 4600rpm. Rugged and simple, the engine was built for sturdiness and long life. Both Uhlenhaut and Nallinger realized that a reliable engine was the name of the game in endurance racing and the 3.0 liter six was that. Although it would receive extensive modification, the final version used in the 300SL closely relied on the original design.

Alfred Neubauer objected strongly to use

the same with Mercedes-Benz 300s that William Lyons had done with the XK-120 Jaguars. The XK-120C had been little more than an aerodynamic body covering slightly modified suspension, lighter frame, and moderately tuned version of an off-the-shelf engine. In Jaguar's case it was the famous double-overhead-cam of this engine. He wanted more horsepower and less weight. He also objected to the standard transmission of the 300, complained about the quality of the brakes, and criticized the diameter of the tires. All of his arguments were just, and each would eventually be addressed by Uhlenhaut and Nallinger, as Neubauer played devil's advocate to their every move.

In the end, Uhlenhaut extracted 170hp from the 300 sedan engine without increasing its displacement, but the 300SL's success would rely as much on engineering as sheer horsepower. In addition to a revised engine, the 300SL would require a lightweight frame and a streamlined body to become a winner. It was indeed Sir William Lyons' formula translated into German.

In building the 300SL, numerous components were taken directly from the 300 sedan. For the front axle, the only modification was holes drilled in the upper spring and shock supports for weight reduction. The gearbox and long-arm shifter were taken from the standard 300 sedan without significant modification. Another unchanged feature was the cast-iron gearbox; Daimler-Benz just added an oil pump and modifed the gear profiles in order to cope with the higher torque.

One area where the sedan's design had little influence was the 300SL's track. Uhlenhaut had this to consider: While a narrow track would help reduce frontal area, the rear axle required a wide track to counter the significant weakness of the swing axle—its propensity (when cornered smartly) to swap ends. Uhlenhaut and his racing drivers knew that a wider rear track was the only way to reduce the swing axle's significant—and undesirable—changes of rear wheel camber. The final result was a compromise: front track was 1340mm or 52.76in and a rear track of 1445mm or 56.89in.

The first few cars built were fitted with five-stud disc wheels, which were replaced as soon as possible by light-alloy rims using a central-locking, knock-off hub with 6.70x15in tires. The choice of tire dimensions had also been a concession. While Neubauer had insisted on 16in tires offering the advantage of lower operating temperatures, the final decision was to stick with the 15in tires from the sedan. This offered twin advantages of lower unsprung weight and a tiny reduction of the swing axle's squirreliness.

In order to achieve the right front-end shape, the straight-six engine had to be tilted 50 degrees to the left, moving the crankshaft to the right of the car's centerline, thus killing the proverbial two birds with one stone. The car became lower and its center of mass was now almost exactly in the center. Another advantage was that this gave the driver more legroom, albeit at the passenger's expense. The final result ensured that the six-cylinder engine could devote more horsepower to speed and less to overcoming the car's aerodynamic drag.

The sleek, rounded contours of the body were a perfect match for Uhlenhaut's tubular spaceframe. Slipping through the air, the 300SL carried no superfluous cargo, no chrome-plated bumpers, no door handles, no outside rear-view mirrors—nothing to increase drag. The wind tunnel revealed a drag factor of 0.25, a figure that car manufacturers find challenging forty years later!

The real heart of the 300 *Sehr Leicht*, which roughly translates as "lightweight," was the 300SL's multi-tube spaceframe, made up of 25x1mm, 25x2mm, and 18x1mm chrome-molybdenum tubes. The entire structure weighed only 181lb with support for the engine, transmission, and rear axle provided by three large, oval crossmembers.

While ideal for a racing car the space-

frame did present certain problems. Racing cars do not ordinarily have to be engineered for practical considerations, such as ease of entry and exit, but there was the possibility that the race car could become the basis for a road-going model, and *here* lay the unique problem Uhlenhaut faced with his spaceframe—which indirectly brought about the car's most revered feature.

In order to provide adequate beam strength, the spaceframe had to be elevated between the wheels, creating a high, wide sill that the occupants had to surmount when entering or leaving the car. This shape pretty well eliminated the use of conventional door design. Uhlenhaut and Chief Designer Karl Wilfert arrived at one in which entry was quite literally through the roof, a large panel hinged at the top which could be lifted straight up. The choice of this design was im-

pelled by Alfred Neubauer's encyclopedic knowledge of the rules. Having studied the pertinent racing codes and regulations, he was unable to discover any prohibition for doors opening and closing upwards. Although there were door disputes during the 1952 racing season, stylist Wilfert was able to prove convincingly that "form follows function" is indeed the best principle of modern design. While the facts may take away some of the romance behind the 300SL, the truth is, the fabled Gullwing door was simply born of necessity.

As a racer, the 300SL was one of the best engineered and perhaps the most comfortably appointed cars ever campaigned by a factory team. The 300SL featured seriously upholstered seats, plus a genuine instrument panel with large speedometer and tachometer. To the left and right of the large four-spoke steering wheel (fitted with a thumb release pivot to provide easier access) there were four smaller circular instruments monitoring the coolant temperature, fuel pressure, oil temperature, and oil pressure. There was no fuel gauge, but a stop-watch lived in the middle of the dashboard. While the 300SL was obviously still a race car, it was unusually refined compared with the typical race cars of the time.

It's not surprising that the 300SL made quite a spectacle in 1952 when arriving in the paddock for the first time. Uhlenhaut's cars went on to dominate the 1952 season for Mercedes-Benz, and with body designer Karl Wilfert's smoothing out of the race car *cum* road car coachwork, the 300SL earned a permanent niche in the pantheon of great sports cars.

The importance of the 300SL to Mercedes-Benz was best summed up in 1988 by Bruno Sacco, current Director of Design for

Daimler-Benz AG. Discussing the role of the 300SL as a competition car based almost entirely on parts bin components, Sacco gave credit where it was due, to Rudolf Uhlenhaut and his team. "The true designers of the 300SL," he wrote, "are to be found among the engineers who, in 1952, were able to put a successful racing car on the circuit. The step from this concept to the standard SL two years later was not very big, and yet remarkably successful." Given the SL's racing pedigree, the production coupes introduced in 1954 were only "slightly civilized," yet designers the world over have declared Uhlenhaut's 300SL as nothing short of remarkable. Concluded Sacco, "The 300SL Gullwing of 1954 can be classified as a virtuoso performance in a symphony of design!"

Although countless accolades have been accorded Uhlenhaut for the 300SL, his achievements at Daimler-Benz after 1952 are equally significant, in particular the champion 300SLR, prepared by Daimler-Benz for the 1954 Grand Prix season.

In later years, Rudolf Uhlenhaut was recognized as an engineer open to new ideas, new concepts, and no prior restraints were sacrosanct under his tenure at Daimler-Benz. In the late 1960s he even took the position that racing was not a necessity to develop new passenger-car ideas. His series of C111 Wankel-powered test cars were created with computer technology and while utilizing concepts other companies applied on the track, the C111s were never entered in wheel-to-wheel combat. Once considered a potential successor to the 300SL, the "Gull-winged" C111s never progressed beyond the prototype stage due to doubts about the Wankel engine. Perhaps it was just as well. The Gullwing design, as history has confirmed, worked only once!

Throughout the 1960s and up until his retirement in 1972, Uhlenhaut's efforts were focused on the development and testing of Mercedes-Benz production cars. His work had a major influence on the design of the 230, 250, and 280SL, the powerful Mercedes-Benz 6.3 and 6.9 models, the ostentatious 600 limousine, and the sleek 450SL.

Those who knew him speak only praise, and despite his many accomplishments and unparalleled skills as both an engineer and driver, Rudolf Uhlenhaut remained an unpretentious man throughout his entire life. One of the most brilliant and colorful people in Mercedes-Benz history, Rudolf Uhlenhaut died in May 1989, at the age of 82.

FROM RACE CARS TO ROAD CAR

TO NEW YORK CITY VIA THE NÜRBURGRING

It seems remarkable that Daimler-Benz could have designed and built the 300SL in less than a year, and then taken the un-proven car into competition and won all but a single race in its first season. The astounding success of the 300SL race cars in the five major events in which they were entered in 1952 is still regarded more than forty years later as one of the finest factory racing efforts in motorsports history.

The first competition trial for the 300SL was Italy's grueling Mille Miglia, held on May 3–4, 1952. Mercedes-Benz entered three cars, chassis numbers 00003/52, 00004/52, and 00005/52. Number 3 was driven by Hermann Lang and entered as starter number 628; car number 4, starter number 623, was driven by Karl Kling, who eventually finished second; and car number 5, starter number 613, was driven by the legendary Rudolf Caracciola, who had won the race twenty-one years earlier at the wheel of a Mercedes-Benz SSK.

While racing manager Alfred Neubauer had already proven to his own satisfaction that the unique design of the 300SL was not in violation of any rules, there was some ap-prehension within Daimler-Benz that the car's Gullwing door design would be protest-ed if Mercedes won. On April 7, 1952, Fritz Nallinger sent a telegram to Neubauer, who was in Italy preparing for the race, asking if indeed a protest might be lodged. Wrote Nallinger: "Have just heard that Italian competitors plan to protest against our body design if we win—stop—You have already clarified the matter with the organizer—Written agreement required—Daimler-Benz Nallinger."

Neubauer was already well ahead of the game. He answered Nallinger the following morning: "The information you have received that 'our competitors will protest if we win' is wrong and inappropriate. Any complaints about vehicle specifications must be submitted at the latest two hours after approval of vehicles (Article 171 of the International Sports Code). No protests or complaints are accepted after the race. Contrary to your assumption, I deliberately have not discussed the subject of body design with the race organizers. I have always told Mr. Uhlenhaut that I will be able to argue our design successfully. So far nobody has criticized our body design, although I have discussed

The 300SL coupe, introduced in 1954 and based on the 1952 race cars, has become one of the benchmark automotive designs of all time.

The 300SL competition cars were the basis for the later production 300SL coupes. However, the first race cars were far simpler in design. The Gullwing doors only extended to the tops of the fenders, just adequate for the driver to clamber over and into the cockpit.
Daimler-Benz AG

the matter for hours with the race steward, Mr. Castagneto, the President of the Italian Sports Association, Mr. Brivio, and his deputy. They have all seen our photos and would certainly have made any comments where appropriate. I fear that any inquiry on my part might be regarded as a sign of weakness and that it would be better to simply enter our cars for approval, trusting that everything is all right."

Neubauer's assessment of the situation was astute, if not purely cunning. In another communiqué to Nallinger he observed that, "Considering we haven't done anything wrong, I suggest that we simply go all out to

have our cars approved, since we haven't broken the rules in any way. Once we have approval, we'll have achieved a breakthrough for all other events, and that, I think, is the most important point. I'm also convinced that they'll have no other choice in the last minute but to accept our cars."

It went exactly as Neubauer had expected; all three cars were allowed to start without protest. Thus began the now famous wheel-to-wheel battle between Mercedes driver Karl Kling and Ferrari's Giovanni Bracco. The two remained close throughout the entire 1,000 mile contest with Kling leading the field at the halfway mark in Rome and into

Florence. Bracco's reckless attack on Kling's position was unrelenting, and he overtook him in the mountain fog between Florence and Bologna, gaining a two-minute lead. Bracco pressed on in the fast stretches after Bologna with his 250MM crossing the finish line in Brescia 4 minutes 32 seconds ahead of Kling's 300SL.

For an untried car against a seasoned competitor, coming in on Ferrari's heels was hardly a disgrace. The Daimler-Benz AG Information Bulletin proclaimed it a triumph: "Finishing second in the toughest race in the history of the Mille Miglia, Daimler-Benz have shown a second time that we are able to design, develop and build a race-worthy car within just a couple of months. This success scored by the 300SL is quite equal to the previously unique achievement in Tripoli with our 1.5 liter race car built within just 8 months. Both the Company and our drivers can be more than satisfied with our successful first try in the world's toughest road race using a car developed from a standard production vehicle."

The second race of the season, the Berne Sports Car Prize, would be the first overall victory for the new race cars. It would be a bittersweet success, however, marred by a near-fatal crash involving Rudolf Caracciola.

Just two weeks after the Mille Miglia, a team of four 300SLs was entered at Berne, Switzerland. Chassis number 00003/52 with Hermann Lang at the wheel; Kling in 00004/

Tail of the first race car with the Gullwing doors ending at the top of the fenders.
Daimler-Benz AG

The second style of competition 300SL featured larger Gullwing doors making entry and exit easier for race drivers in a hurry during pitstops.
Daimler-Benz AG

52; Caracciola once again in 00005/52; and Fritz Riess in the cockpit of 00002/52, the second model in the first series of the 300SL. Refitted with new, larger doors, which extended down to the middle of the fenders, number 2 became the prototype for the second series ranging from chassis numbers 00006/52 to 00009/52. Various reinforcements had also been added, increasing the dry weight of the car by some 44lb.

The revised door design was the result of Neubauer's exacting research into the rules and regulations for each race in which the 300SL was entered. Although they would be approved at Berne, the rules for Le Mans, coming up in June, expressly stated that cars

entered must have a *bona fide* touring-car body. Wrote Neubauer, "the 24 Hours of Le Mans is really an endurance test for production cars. So I think we must strictly distinguish

between Le Mans and the 1,000 Miles."

Once again his strategy paid off. Berne afforded him the opportunity to find out from the sports commissioners whether larger doors would be accepted in Le Mans, since this would at least refute the claim that the 300SL was simply not a touring car due to its doors alone.

Practice sessions in Berne already had Ferraris pitted against Mercedes. Swiss driver W. P. Daetwyler was far ahead of the pack in his 4.1 liter Ferrari, setting up a record lap time of 2 minutes 55.6 seconds, equal to an average speed of 92.534mph. Then came four Mercedes only moments apart, Kling with a lap time of 3:00.1 minutes, Lang with 3:03.3, Caracciola with 3:04.1, and Riess with the new 300SL posting 3:07.7. Among the remaining fifteen cars there were two Aston Martins, a pair of Lancia Aurelias, two more Ferraris, three Jaguars, two BMWs, an HWM, a lone Cisitalia, and a one-off race car built by driver Jean Studer.

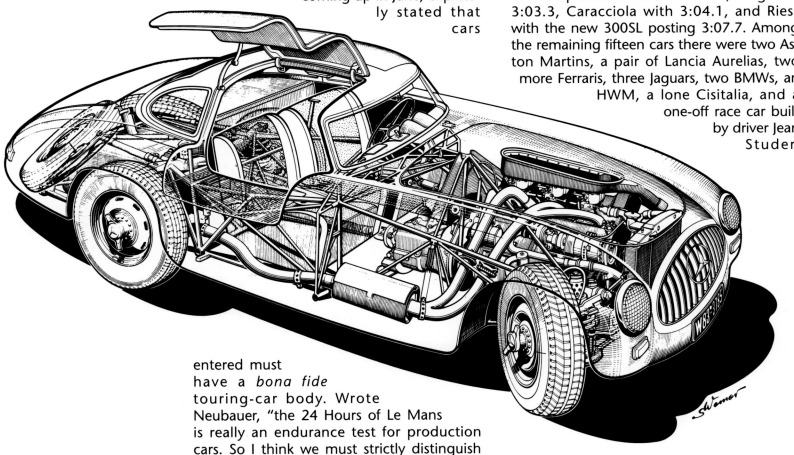

At the start of the race, Daetwyler's Ferrari retired almost immediately with a broken propshaft, relinquishing the lead to Caracciola, who was passed by Lang on the next lap. With the Germans in the first two positions, Kling moved up by the fifth lap along with Riess who had started from the last position on the grid. Within minutes the cars from Stuttgart occupied the first four places. Then it happened.

This is how Rudolf Caracciola described his crash from the hospital when interviewed by the daily newspaper *Pirmasenser Zeitung* on May 30, 1952: "It was in lap 13. I was approaching *Forsthaus Bend* at 190 km/h and was just about to shift down. I put my foot lightly on the brake pedal and suddenly the brake shoes on the right side of the car got stuck. This forced me to the side of the road and I obviously wasn't able to steer clear at

A shot of the 300SL that is seldom seen: the bare spaceframe with engine block in place. Photo was taken at the werke in 1952.
Daimler-Benz AG

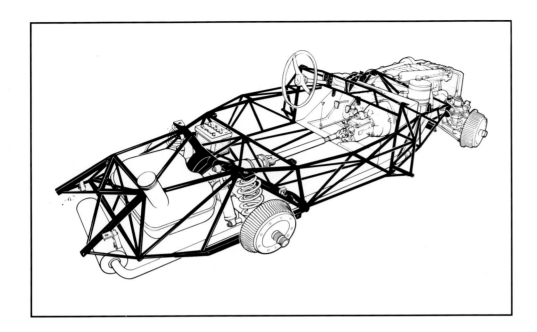

this kind of speed. So all I could do was press my legs against the floor, trying not to fly out over the windscreen. Then I hit a 20-meter-high ash tree at the edge of the forest, just a meter off the track. It was terrible, I tell you. I was tossed around like a leaf in a storm, I felt something go snap in my right thigh, and I was covered by the shattered windscreen. The ash-tree crashed down on to the road and then everything was quiet...."

Although his fractured femur healed quite quickly, one of the greatest drivers of all time decided after this accident (his third severe crash) to retire.

The winner of the race was Karl Kling followed by Hermann Lang in second. Third place was Riess, one lap behind the leaders, with two Aston Martins and the two Lancia

Drawing of the spaceframe
chassis fitted with engine
and driveline.
Daimler-Benz AG

Layout of the 300SL roadster
spaceframe as shown in the
1963 brochure.
Frank Barrett Collection

Mercedes-Benz 300SL

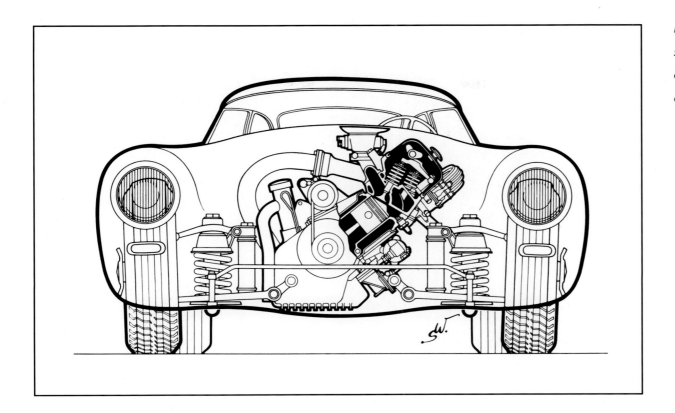

Layout of the 300SL engine showing the slanted position of the cylinders relative to the oilpan. **Daimler-Benz AG**

Aurelias following.

Despite Caracciola's misfortune, the sweeping first through third finish had proven the SL's capabilities. For all intents, the Mille Miglia and Berne Sports Car Prize had been only trials in preparation for the most important race in Europe, the 24 Heures du Mans.

Neubauer's strategy for Le Mans was simply to rule out even the slightest risk right from the start. "Winning a race is 99 percent good preparation and only 1 percent luck," wrote Neubauer. And this is precisely how Mercedes tackled the challenge in France.

Fritz Riess' car had already proven in Berne that there would be no problem with the regulations at Le Mans. Now, Neubauer

had a new surprise for the competition, which by now believed that they had seen everything Mercedes had to throw at them in Berne. Suddenly, here was another.

In its development, there had been a third design study for the 300SL, which employed a unique roof-mounted air brake. This was fitted to 00006/52 for the practice sessions at Le Mans, and upon its appearance caused a wave of panic to spread among Mercedes' competitors.

When applied, the air brake would flip upright, creating greater downforce on the rear wheels when braking and without any pressure being taken off the front wheels. The brake flap also had a stabilizing effect on the car's handling, allowing the SL to brake and handle more aggressively through corners.

At Le Mans, the air brake was able to pro-

vide an amazing reduction of speed at the end of the long Mulsanne straight, however, the practice sessions also proved that the design had a structural problem. The support brackets for the air brake were simply not strong enough to withstand the excessive forces created by its deployment. After a few hours, metal fatigue would have likely torn the air brake from the car. To the relief of Mercedes' rivals, it was not used in the race. The air brake would, however, reappear in 1956 on the championship 300SLR.

Mercedes entered Le Mans with three new cars: 00007/52, starter number 21, driven by Hermann Lang and Fritz Riess; 00008/52, starter number 22, with Karl Kling and Hans Klenk; and Theo Helfrich joining forces with co-driver Norbert Niedermayer in 00009/52, with starter number 20. All three cars featured the new larger Gullwing door design.

Hopes of a one-two-three sweep were dashed when Kling retired early in the race with a defective generator. After twenty-four hours of grueling racing, Lang and Riess came in first to clinch the title, followed by Helfrich and Niedermayer in second.

Although Mercedes was triumphant, the victory had taken far more than the 1 percent of luck Neubauer's formula prescribed. Quite a bit more. Five Ferraris and one Gordini had

The 300SL engine was crowned by the beautiful, cast-aluminum air intake pipes; the exhaust pipes snaked down below the intake manifold.
Daimler-Benz AG

Opposite page
Factory workers assemble a transmission for the race car. Note the long-neck shifter that was taken from the 300 sedans.
Daimler-Benz AG

The other side of the 300SL engine was a maze of plumbing originating from the fuel-injection pump.
Daimler-Benz AG

achieved faster lap times than the Mercedes, but were forced out of the race by technical problems or spent too much time in the pits. And Frenchman Pierre Levegh's Talbot had been ahead of the Germans until the twenty-third hour, before losing oil and consequently suffering a broken connecting rod. Nevertheless, a win by endurance was all the more sweet for Daimler-Benz. Their competitors had broken; the Mercedes had not.

After three races abroad, Daimler-Benz felt it was high time to present the 300SL on a German racetrack, and Alfred Neubauer chose the Nürburgring Sports Car Prize to be held on August 3rd, 1952, as their premiere event.

There was one problem, however: The race was just 141 miles long, and the Gullwing coupes were too heavy compared to the lighter-weight roadsters they would be running against. Neubauer and Uhlenhaut had four of the SL coupes quickly converted into lightweight roadsters. Chassis number 00006/52 would be driven by Theo Helfrich and entered as starter number 23. The rebodied car was finished in silver and trimmed with distinctive green paintwork around the headlights. Fritz Riess was given chassis number 00009/52, and this car featured red paint around the headlights. Riess would be starter number 22. Also converted into a roadster, the winning car from Le Mans, 00007/52, was entered with starter number 21 and factory ace Hermann Lang at the wheel.

Interestingly enough, the fourth car, 00002/52, driven by Karl Kling, was actually entered in the Nürburgring race twice. The car entered practice on July 31, fitted with a supercharged engine that moved the SL up into the 8.0 liter category. Neubauer's plan was to test the experimental 300SLK ("K" for Kompressor) during practice, as entry number 31, and if the SLK proved faster than the normally aspirated cars, convert two additional cars, giving them starter numbers 32 and 33, which he had already reserved. If not, the standard engine with three Solex carburetors could be replaced in 00002/52, and the car was already entered as starter number 24.

The number 00002 chassis had been used as a practice car in the Mille Miglia, and was also used at Berne as a standby. This was now to be Neubauer's experimental car. When it was converted into a roadster, Mercedes not only fitted it with the supercharged M197 engine, but also shortened the wheelbase to 86.6in for the sake of even better handling on the difficult Nürburgring racetrack. However, during the practice sessions the M197 engine did not provide the benefits Uhlenhaut and Neubauer had hoped for.

Kling first lapped the circuit in 10:24.8 with a standard 300SL. He then took the Kompressor car out and pushing it to the limit turned a time of 10:25.1. In spite of an additional 45hp, the single-stage Roots-su-

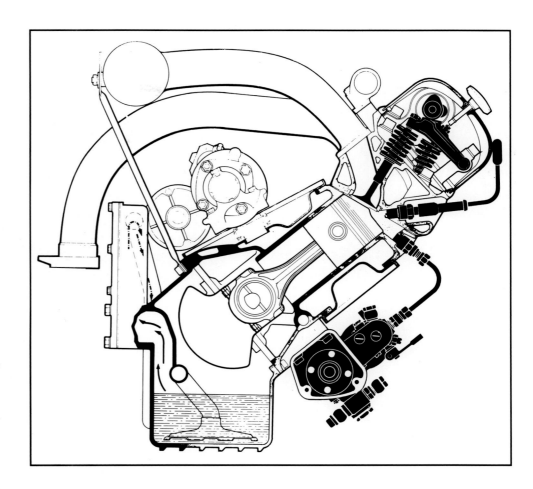

Layout of the 300SL engine.

Daimler-Benz AG

percharged SLK proved no faster than a normally aspirated 300SL.

Rudolf Uhlenhaut quickly ascertained the problem. It was not the engine but the car. "With a normal swing axle," he explained, "the inner wheel becomes increasingly light in fast, narrow bends and may even lift off the road due to the high point of rotation of this kind of axle, preventing you from cornering smoothly and quickly and thus ultimately reducing your speed. Probably, this is the reason for our disappointing lap times at Nürburgring. While acceleration was admittedly better on the relatively short straights, this was barely enough to make up for the

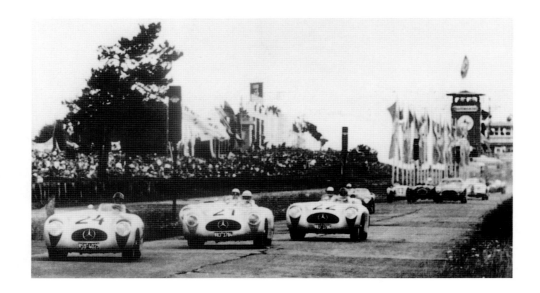

time lost in bends."

In the Nürburgring race all four cars were equipped with carbureted engines. Kling's short-wheelbase 300SL was leading the field when his car swerved out of control on a patch of oil. He nevertheless remained in second place behind Hermann Lang, who scored his second victory after Le Mans. With Riess and Helfrich finishing third and fourth, Mercedes swept the race. The Press Department proudly announced on August 3: "Starting for the first time on German soil, the 300SL was once again an overwhelming success. All four cars put up a great show to thrill the 250,000 spectators." Their press release closed by stating, "We believe that this

All four 300SL competition roadsters on their way to a sweep of the first through fourth places at the Nürburgring, August 3, 1952.

Right
The 300SL fuel-injection system.

Opposite page
In terms of sales competition, Porsche was the 300SL's number one rival. The 356 Speedster was far less expensive and only capable of about 100mph, but it appealed to many more buyers in postwar Europe than did the Mercedes.

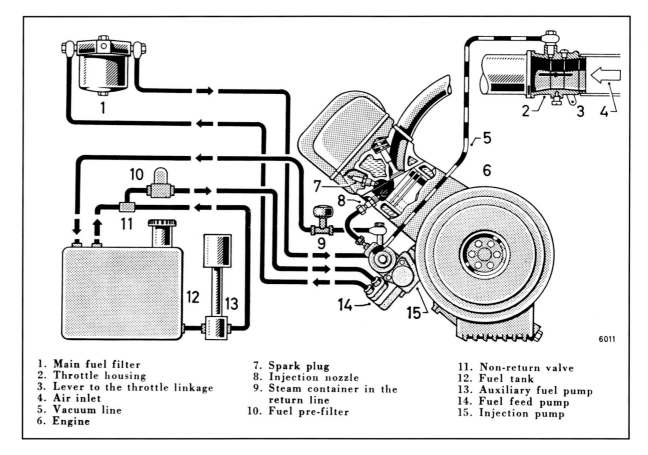

6011

1. Main fuel filter
2. Throttle housing
3. Lever to the throttle linkage
4. Air inlet
5. Vacuum line
6. Engine
7. Spark plug
8. Injection nozzle
9. Steam container in the return line
10. Fuel pre-filter
11. Non-return valve
12. Fuel tank
13. Auxiliary fuel pump
14. Fuel feed pump
15. Injection pump

Car number 00007/52 (#21)
driven by Hermann Lang and
Fritz Riess on the way to victory
in the 1952 24 Heures du Mans.
Daimler-Benz AG

Opposite page

*The chief competition to the
300SL came from Maranello,
Italy. Enzo Ferrari took the
racing world by storm in the
early years following World
War II, and it was the Ferrari
that Mercedes-Benz would
measure itself against. Ferrari's
Vignale-bodied 212 Inter
had won the Carrera Pan-
Americana, and was not only
priced commensurately with
the 300SL but was its equal
in performance.*

excellent result will promote the sales of all Mercedes-Benz cars."

At Daimler-Benz, plans were already under way for a new and more powerful race car to succeed the 300SL. Toward the end of August 1952, Mercedes announced in an official statement that it had now reached all of its sporting objectives, and that the 300SLs would be withdrawn from competition. Then came the phone call from the Daimler-Benz importer in Mexico, explaining about the upcoming Carrera PanAmericana.

With added prodding from DBAG's US importer, Max Hoffman, the factory was convinced to enter the 300SLs in the great Mexican road race. This would be the car's

Tire changes were frequent in the grueling 1952 Carrera PanAmericana. Neither the cars nor the drivers had been prepared for the rough Mexican roads.
Daimler-Benz AG

Production SLs were campaigned by privateer drivers throughout the world. Here, a stock coupe without bumpers challenges the superfast Spa-Francorchamps circuit in 1954.
Daimler-Benz AG

final and most incredible challenge.

Running from Ciudad Juarez on the US-Mexican border over a distance of 3,130km or 1,941 miles to El Ocotal on the Guatemala frontier, the first Carrera PanAmericana took place in 1950. The winner was American Hershel McGriff driving an Oldsmobile 88. He covered the distance in a winning time (driving time only) of 27 hours, 34 minutes, 25 seconds. The next race in 1951 marked the year of the Ferraris, with Piero Taruffi and Luigi Chinetti clinching the title at the wheel of their Vignale-bodied 212 Inter, followed by teammates Alberto Ascari and Luigi Villoresi also in a 212 Inter.

The thought of challenging the Ferraris in the Mexican desert was almost intoxicating. Neubauer's competition department rallied to the occasion handling the team's preparation for the Carrera with extraordinary efficiency. For the trip, two 3.5-ton transporters, a staff of thirty-five engineers and mechanics, as well as three racing cars, plus a standby car, were sent to Mexico.

All four 300SLs eventually participated in the race. Car 00005/52, which had been rebuilt after Caracciola's shunt, was entered as starter number 3 and driven by the team of Hermann Lang and Erwin Grupp. Car 00008/52, the standby car at the Nürbur-

Converted from a roadster back into a coupe for the 1952 Carrera PanAmericana was number 00008/52. It was driven by veterans Karl Kling and Hans Klenk. The car looked somewhat less elegant after the race, having collided head-on with a vulture, after which the car was fitted with steel bars over the windshield.

Triumphant in the 1952 Carrera PanAmericana, an exultant Mercedes-Benz team poses with the winning car. Pictured left to right, Neubauer, Geiger, Fitch, Klenk, Kling, Lang and Grupp.
Daimler-Benz AG

Karl Kling (right) and Hans Klenk inspect the shattered windshield of their car during the first leg of the Carrera PanAmericana from Tuxtla Gutiérrez to Oaxaca.
Daimler-Benz AG

gring, was converted from a roadster back into a coupe and entered as starter number 4, driven by veterans Karl Kling and Hans Klenk. The roadster with chassis number 00009/52 retained its open body and was driven by American John Fitch, who had convinced Neubauer of his skills during a trial session at the Nürburgring; Fitch's co-driver would be Eugen Geiger. The standby car was the Nürburgring winner, chassis number 00007/52, driven this time by journalist Günter Molter, who later became the Daimler-Benz Press Manager.

Studying the regulations of the race, Neubauer had found that there was no 3.0 liter category in Mexico, so the engine bore

would have to be increased from 85 to 86mm (3.35 to 3.39in), to raise engine capacity to 3.1 liters.

One of the unanticipated problems in Mexico—among many that would surface throughout the race—was tires. The roads were entirely different from those for the Italian Mille Miglia and the prepared surfaces of the various European venues where the cars had competed. Continental shipped 300 tires for the race, some of thick-tread Nürburgring design for twisty, high-wear tracks, others with the Avus pattern with thinner tread rubber. Quick experience on the Mexican roads proved the Avus pattern as the better of the two.

Once again, Mercedes-Benz was facing its most formidable Italian competitors, Ferrari and Lancia. Ferrari had entered four of their large 340 Mexico and America models, plus several 212 Exports and a 250 S driven by Giovanni Bracco and Gino Bronzoni. Three Lancia B20 Aurelias also had top-notch drivers at the wheel: Felice Bonetto, Giulio Casabianca, and Umberto Maglioli in a supercharged B20.

Considering this kind of challenge, it's no surprise that Alfred Neubauer wanted more

time to prepare for the race. But the starting date was definite, November 19, 1952.

Always the strategist, Neubauer decided to hold back at the beginning of the race into Mexico City. His plan was to get his cars to the capital in good shape and then stage an attack on the high-speed routes that were to follow. This proved a wise decision. The first leg from Tuxtla Gutiérrez to Oaxaca was fraught with unexpected problems.

Unlike any race Mercedes-Benz drivers had ever competed in, Mexico had its own unique "charm." People stood right alongside the road course—dangerously close—as did a variety of local animals, attracted by the noise. Hermann Lang was the first to encounter this problem when he piled his SL into a dog, bending the front section of the car and possibly damaging the steering. Still, it was Karl Kling's head-on confrontation with

a vulture that is regarded as the most momentous "collision" of any auto race in modern history. Recalled Kling, "There was a huge bang as if a grenade had just exploded, then there was a gaping hole in the windscreen and co-driver Hans Klenk was bleeding all over, the vulture torn to pieces and dying in the back of the passenger compartment."

Klenk was treated by first-aid people at the next tire stop and a strong iron grid was fitted in front of the windscreen; in addition, the car took on three new spare tires. Despite this misfortune, Kling was in third position at the end of this leg, with the other cars coming in seventh and eighth.

In Mexico City, the longer final drive ratio Fitch had used from the beginning was fitted in the two coupes by Prat Motors. By now the three Mercedes were second, third, and fourth, but Ferrari's Bracco was far out in the lead.

The outcome of the race was decided on the seventh leg when Bracco's Ferrari retired with a damaged differential and two broken valve shafts. The Mercedes team also suffered a loss of its own, though not mechanical in nature. John Fitch was disqualified at the start in Parral. In his account of the incident, Fitch said that he had felt something wrong with the steering and front suspension alignment after pulling away from the start, and some 200 meters down the road, turned back to have the car re-checked by the mechanics.

The rules stated quite clearly, however, that no repairs were allowed during the race itself—and that was the end of the Carrera PanAmericana for John Fitch. At the time, it seemed of little consequence to Neubauer who had his hands full just trying to keep track of the remaining two cars, now far in the lead and pushing speeds of up to 155mph. He chartered a DC 3 spotter plane to keep an eye on the race from above, but Neubauer still wasn't able to match the speed of the SLs.

The standard order from Max Hoffman was a car in traditional Mercedes-Benz racing colors—silver gray exterior with traditional blue gaberdine plaid and tex-leather upholstery.

The two-piece leather luggage set was an option that many 300SL owners purchased. With little or no room in the trunk, the specially designed suitcases fit perfectly on the shelf behind the seats.

Opposite page
Clean lines were the hallmark of the 300SL design. The roofline swept back to let air roll off and flow gently over the rear decklid. As an aerodynamic study, the 300SL was far ahead of its contemporaries.

The standard fuel-injected 3.0 liter inline six-cylinder 300SL engine was rated at 215bhp at 5800rpm with a 3.35x3.46in bore and stroke and 8.55:1 compression ratio. Cars equipped with the standard 3.64:1 final drive ratio had a top speed of 146mph. Options included a 9.5:1 compression ratio and competition camshaft increasing output to approximately 240bhp. With the optional 3.25:1 final drive ratio, 300SLs could reach a top speed of 161mph.

Mercedes finally clinched their one-two victory in Ciudad Juarez. Together with co-driver Hans Klenk, Karl Kling won the race at an average speed of 102.1mph, with Hermann Lang and Erwin Grupp finishing second. This was a triumphant victory indeed, as only thirty-nine out of the ninety-two starters even made it to the finish line. Kling had broken virtually every PanAmericana record. His winning time was 18 hours, 51 minutes, and 19 seconds.

The old saying, "race on Sunday, sell on Monday" was never more appropriate than after the PanAmericana. Within a week after the race, Mercedes-Benz received more than 400 orders for the 300SL model, although its price in Mexico would have been more than 115,000 pesos—at the time about $13,500 if Mercedes had been offering 300SLs for sale.

Not since Italy had Mercedes-Benz SLs seen another competitor cross the finish line before them. In just five events, the 300SL

Opposite page

An early 300SL in the second series, noted by the straight star and barrel grille design. Unless color choice was specified by the purchaser, the cars came from the factory finished in the standard Daimler-Benz exterior color of silver gray.

Unless one were driving a new Ferrari in the 1950s, this was the most frequently seen view of a 300SL. They were the fastest production automobiles available in 1954. While most cars of the era were pushing hard to sustain a top speed of 100mph, a 300SL could reach that speed in third gear.

Countless stories have been told about the creation of the 300SL, the most famous and closest to the truth involves Max Hoffman, the American and Canadian importer for Mercedes-Benz.

Perhaps no one in postwar automotive history did more to bring foreign cars to US shores than Hoffman. He always knew what would sell, and it was at his insistence that Daimler-Benz built not one but two new sports cars for 1954: The 300SL and its smaller sibling, the 190SL roadster.

Allegedly, Hoffman convinced Daimler-Benz management to build the 300SL by placing a firm order for 1,000 cars to be delivered as soon as possible. This, of course, has proven to be a fabulous myth. Heinz Hoppe, the Daimler-Benz US representative, later President of Daimler-Benz of North America and finally Board Member for Sales in Stuttgart, cannot recall the now-legendary 1,000 car order. "Maxie Hoffman was an ingenious salesman with an incredible feeling for anything that would go in the market. He was the man who introduced Porsche, Jaguar and Ferrari to the States. But his biggest and most successful deal was a contract with BMW granting him the sales rights for the Bavarian marque for an unlimited period. That contract ultimately cost BMW a lot of money when they decided to set up their own sales and distribution organization. Being a shrewd businessman, Maxie was wise enough not to sign a contract for 1,000 unsold cars. It is true, of course, that he really knew the market and that he was constantly urging us to build the car his rich customers were clamoring for." And build it they did.

Preparations for the launch of the 300SL started in the spring of 1953 with the car's world debut scheduled to take place at the New York International Motor Sports Show the following February.

had gone from obscurity to the most talked about and desirable race car in the world. There were orders for 300SLs coming in from all over the world and American importer Max Hoffman was pressing Daimler-Benz management to build a production version of the car, which he believed could be sold by the thousands.

At the same time, Uhlenhaut and his engineering team were working on an improved version of the 300SL for the 1953 season, despite company policy to the contrary. While at least one and possibly two prototypes were built, they were never raced. However, the 1953 model, with a wider, lower nose, larger Gullwing doors, a lower roofline, air extraction slots in the front fender, and a new Bosch fuel-injected engine under its hood, would become the final link between race and road car.

New York City in the throes of winter hardly seems the place to have a world debut but the major American auto shows—Los Angeles, Detroit, Chicago and New York—have traditionally been staged in the winter months. In the 1950s, New York's International Motor Sports Show was considered one of America's premiere events, and it was here on February 6, 1954, that the 300SL was introduced to the world. It would mark the first time in Daimler-Benz history that a new model would be shown outside of the country before it was introduced in Germany, a testament to the importance of the US market, and perhaps to the influence Max Hoffman had with Daimler-Benz.

Heinz Hoppe later said that people in Germany and Europe were so poor at the time of the 300SL's introduction that Daimler-Benz could hardly imagine selling the car in its part of the world, especially at the price Mercedes-Benz would have to ask. "We charged twice the price of a Corvette or a Jaguar—only a Ferrari had roughly the same price-tag," said Hoppe. It was a car intended for the US market first and foremost.

Indeed, most 300SLs were sold in the United States. "About 80 percent of the 1,400 Gullwings and some 70 percent of the 1,858 roadsters went to the States," said Klaus Kienle, who operated one of the most renowned restoration workshops in Rutesheim near Stuttgart.

The production cars, while different than their racebred predecessors, had an unmistakable resemblance. They featured the same suspension as the racing model, with only the track having been changed to 54.60in up front and 56.50in at the rear. The road-going 300SL continued to use the 300 sedan's recirculating-ball steering linked to three-piece track rods and requiring two turns of the wheel from lock to lock. The first

151 cars were fitted with ZF worm steering, and the first fifty retained the curved long-neck shifter used on the 300SL race cars and 300 Series sedans.

In only a year, Daimler-Benz had converted a race car into a practical GT coupe for everyday use, a thoroughbred sports car combining the performance of the 1952 racing model with the luxury, comfort, and quality of a Daimler-Benz 300 Series sedan. It was a car capable of road speeds that were truly sensational in 1954 and are still impressive today.

Comparing some of the most popular road cars of the early 1950s, a Volkswagen Beetle could reach 71mph, a 356 Porsche was able to achieve about 100mph, and a Ferrari works competition car near 150mph. The 300SL could attain a top speed of up to 161mph with appropriate gearing.

Within the first year, a total of 166 cars were built, with the majority, 125, sold through Max Hoffman's New York City and Los Angeles, California, dealerships.

Among prominent 300SL owners in 1954 were King Hussein II of Jordan, King Baudouin of Belgium, the Duke of Edinburgh, the Ali Khan and Saddrudin Khan, Constantin of Greece, Argentinean dictator Juan Peron, film stars Mel Farrar, Sophia Loren, and Zsa Zsa Gabor. Wealthy American and European businessmen accounted for the majority of 300SL sales between 1954 and 1957. Among them Briggs Cunningham, Carl Kiekhaefer of Mercury Marine, David Brown of Aston Martin fame, the DuPont family, and a host of privateer racers the world over, who took the production 300SL into sports car club competition throughout the 1950s and early 1960s.

More than any other sports car of its era, the 300SL Gullwing coupe was a genuine sensation—a car that has survived the greatest test of all, the test of time.

THE 300SL COUPE

ON ROAD AND TRACK

No sooner had 300SL owners taken delivery of their cars then they were being entered in sports car club competition. At Pebble Beach, the race through the pines bore witness to a new champion in the over 1500cc class, the Mercedes-Benz 300SL, skillfully driven to victory around the Monterey Peninsula by Tony Settember.

Considered at the time "the most challenging course in America," the 1956 Cypress Point Handicap at Pebble Beach saw a trio of 300SLs entered. Driver Rudy Cleye, who had had an unbroken series of wins throughout the 1956 season, suffered damage to his car prior to the April 21 race, and took over the 300SL Paul O'Shea had cam-

Much of the original 300SL race car design from 1952 carried over into the production version introduced in 1954.

Opposite page

For the early 1950s, the 300SL Gullwing was the most aerodynamically efficient production car on the road. The coupe's sleek body lines and lower wind resistance gave it an edge in sports car club competition against rivals that were more powerful but less aerodynamic.

The Gullwing's greenhouse
(roof and window design)
centered itself deep within the
body, with fenders extending
well beyond the width of the
roofline. It was a perspective
with which few sports cars
have been endowed.

Opposite page
*The classic 300SL pose with
Gullwing doors raised.*

Simplicity can be elegant. The 300SL instrument panel was neither gaudy nor understated. All of the controls and instruments were of modest size and smartly trimmed with chrome accents or bezels. The only shortcoming may have been in leaving the radio components exposed behind the leather-trimmed fascia.

Opposite page
Decked out in the optional leather upholstery and trim, this 300SL coupe is the epitome of sporting luxury with its matching leather luggage, designed and manufactured by Baisch to fit on the parcel shelf behind the seats. Luggage was offered in matching leather or covered in vinyl with pigskin leather corners.

10. Accelerator pedal.

11. Tommy for supplementary ventilation.

12. Clock: the clock is set by turning the button at the right.

13. Oil thermometer.

14. Cooling water thermometer.

15. Steering wheel: the steering wheel can be folded down after the securing lever (16) has been released.

16. Securing lever of steering wheel.

17. Button for signal horns.

18. Control lever for distance light signal system, it is installed only upon request and against extra charge.

19. Rear view mirror, it can be folded back to anti-dazzle position to prevent dazzling from vehicles coming from behind.

20. Ash tray: pull out to empty. Lower part can be taken off by pressing at the sides.

21. Sun vizor.

22. Reading lamp, at the same time entrance light. It is switched on or over by turning the light stop.

Light stop closed: lamp switched off.

Light stop half open: entrance light, the lamp is switched on by a door contact switch which is actuated when the driver's door is opened and lights up as long as this door remains open.

Light stop fully opened: reading lamp; the lamp remains lighted.

When getting out of the car, the light stop should always be set to "entrance light".

Driver's Seat

1. Hand brake lever.

2. Tommy screw for hand brake adjustment.

3. Tommy for engine hood fastener, pull handle to open engine hood.

4. Control lever for direction indicators, push upwards to switch on left flashlight and down for right one.

5. Control lever of windscreen rinsing system, it is installed only upon request and against extra charge.

6. Gear shift lever, 4 forward gears, baulked synchromesh, 1 reverse gear.

7. Foot dimmer switch: push down to switch from "dimmed" to "full" again. The blue signal lamp at the instrument panel indicates the distance light is switched on. See p. 10.

8. Clutch pedal.

9. Brake pedal.

paigned throughout 1955. Cleye experienced engine problems with the O'Shea car early on, and after briefly sharing the lead with Settember and the 1956 Corvette of Dr. Dick Thompson, was forced to drop back.

The presence of 300SLs at motorsport events across the United States and throughout Europe in 1955 and 1956 was focusing as much attention on Mercedes as the factory's own racing efforts had in 1952. Daimler-Benz offered support to individuals campaigning their cars by providing factory mechanics to look after their needs, and at the more important races, even Karl Kling and Alfred Neubauer could be found in attendance. The factory may have withdrawn

from competition, but the number of production 300SLs being raced by privateers more than made up for it.

In Europe, 300SLs were entered in almost every major race of the 1955 and 1956 season. In the 1955 Mille Miglia, John Fitch and Oliver Gendebien won their class and finished fifth overall. Gendebien was also victorious in both the Liège-Rome-Liège and Alpine rallies. W. I. Tak drove his 300SL to victory in the Tulip Rally, Werner Engle won the European Touring Car Championship, Armando Zampiero, the Italian Sports-Car-Driver's Championship, and in America, Paul O'Shea claimed the 1955 SCCA Class Championship. In 1956, Prince Metternich finished

Instrument panel

1. Revolution counter.
2. Blue distance control light; lights up as long as the distance light is switched on.
3. Speedometer indicating the total and daily mileage covered. The daily mileage meter can be returned to O position by pulling the pull knob (4).
4. Pull knob for returning the daily mileage meter to position O.
5. Signal lamp control light.
6. Ignition timing adjustment.
7. Fuel gauge with "full" and "reserve" marking.
8. Oil pressure gauge; indicates only if the engine is running.
9. White starting control light; lights up as long as the choke is pulled.
10. Charging control light; if the electrical system is in order, then it lights up after the key has been inserted in the ignition lock; it goes out if the engine has exceeded the idle running speed (normal driving).
11. Cooling water temperature gauge. The cooling water temperature should not rise above the red limit mark.
12. Oil temperature gauge.
13. Pull switch for the auxiliary fuel pump; to actuate it, pull out, after which a control light in the switch will light up as long as the pump is in operation. It is necessary to actuate the pump if
    (a) the engine should be started in a warm condition;
    (b) the fuel is drawing to an end. The pump conveys the remaining contents of the tank to the engine.
14. Lever for the ventilation of the left side of the windscreen. Lever folded back: closed.
15. Lever for the ventilation of the left side of the leg room. Lever folded back: closed.

16. Pull knob "start". Pulling out switches on the starting device of the injection pump; the white control lamp (9) remains lighted for as long as the start button is pulled out.
17. Pull knob for instrument panel lighting: this is switched on if the rotary switch is set in position 1 or 2 and this pull knob is pulled out.
18. Parking light selector switch. The right or left parking lights light up according to whether it is turned right or left (no centre position). The parking lights are switched on by turning the light selector switch (19) to the left.
19. Light selector switch; 4 positions:

Neutral position (control knob vertical):	"Day driving"; if the ignition lock (20) is set on "driving", the following appliances can be operated: starter control lamp, windscreen wiper, signal horns, fuel gauge, auxiliary fuel pump, cigar lighter, brake light, defroster when the car is standing still, blinker and if it is built-in the distance light blinking system.
Turned from neutral until the I. stop on the right (1):	The following appliances are then switched on: licence plate lighting, tail light, parking light, instrument panel lighting, and after engaging the reverse gear, the reverse drive lamp, if one is installed. In addition, the "day-time consumers" as listed above can be set in operation.
Turned until the II. stop on the right (2):	The distance or dimmed light – according to the position of the dimmer switch – is switched on in addition to (1).
Turned from neutral to the I. stop on the left:	Only the parking lights – the right or the left one according to the position of the parking light selector switch (18) – are switched on; all other exterior lights are switched off.

The fog lamps, which are only built in upon special request and at a surcharge, are also switched on through the light selector switch, which is then turned to position (1) and pulled out.

20. Ignition lock and starter switch. Turning the key to position 1 switches on the electrical system, flexible continued turning to stop 2 – at the same time, the key should be lightly turned forward – switches on the starter motor.

    After the engine starts up, immediately release the key which will then return to stop 1.

21. Two-stage pull knob for the windscreen wiper unit. Pulled out completely: the wiper blades move slowly; half pulled out: the wiper blades move quickly. After switching off, the wiper blades automatically return to their initial position.
22. Control lever for the temperature in the right part of the car. Left position: heating switched off; right position: heating fully opened.
23. Control lever for the temperature in the left part of the car. Position left: heating switched off; position right: heating fully opened.
24. Push button switch for the signal horns.
25. Electrical cigar-lighter: press the button for a few seconds, until the coil glows red.
26. Pull switch for the blowers of the defroster for stationary car. Pulling out switches on the blowers, whereby a control lamp in the pull switch remains lighted for as long as the blowers are in operation.
27. Lever for the ventilation of the right side of the windscreen. Lever folded back: closed.
28. Lever for the ventilation of the right side of the leg room. Lever folded back: closed.

Explanation of the 300SL instrument panel from the owners manual.
Daimler-Benz AG

sixth in the Mille Miglia, the team of Shock and Moll won the Acropolis, and the European Rally Championship, and Sestriére rallies, Stirling Moss finished second in the Tour de France, and Willy Mairesse won the tough Liège-Rome-Liège contest.

It came as no surprise to Daimler-Benz when production versions of the 300SL found their way into club-sanctioned motorsports events. The production cars had been accepted by the FIA for international competition in Group 2, middle section, also called the Grand Turismo Class, and almost immediately there arose a demand for a special competition version of the 300SL.

Daimler-Benz was more than willing to meet the needs of drivers who deemed a 300SL the vehicle with which to challenge the Ferraris, Aston Martins, and Allards wending their way through the pines at Pebble Beach, across sun-baked ribbons of concrete at the Palm Springs airport, and at racing venues all across America.

The all-aluminum coupes were built in 1955 and 1956. As a matter of record, *all* 300SL coupes had aluminum hoods, trunk lids, rocker panels, and door skins; the rest of the body was steel. The lighter, all-aluminum cars were custom built at the factory as special orders and were additionally fitted with plexiglass windows and backlights to further reduce

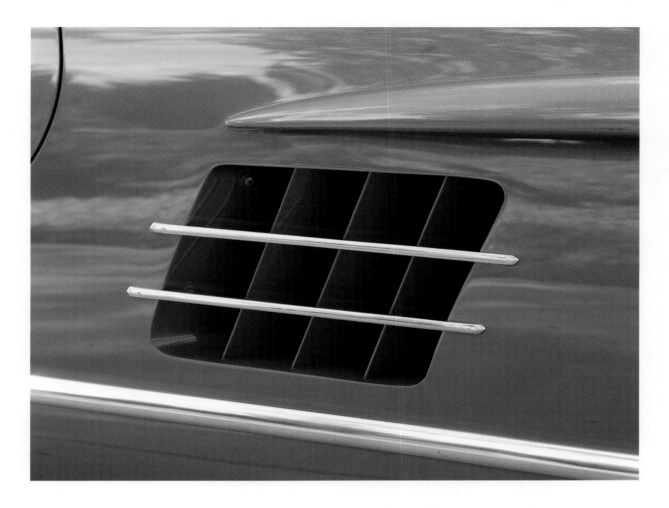

weight; the windshields were still glass. The standard production coupe weighed 2,849lb dry; the alloy cars, 2,669lb. Although 180lb lighter, the alloy SL was still remarkably heavy for a race car. On the track, however, weight hardly seemed to be a disadvantage. These splendid cars gained the upper hand with their trim, wind-cheating aerodynamic profile.

Engines supplied with the alloy coupes were equipped with a competition camshaft; the standard camshaft had an outlet stroke of 0.13in, the sports version 0.33in. The cars were also fitted with higher-rated coil springs, stiffer shocks, and Dunlop racing tires. The brakes were taken from the 1952 race cars, the only difference being that the Al-Fin brake drums had somewhat larger fins for production reasons. Drivers planning to race their cars had six extra-large ventilation holes drilled into the rear panel of the front brake drums, covered by hoods leading to the outside to provide quicker dissipation of brake heat. The race-modified models were also fitted with steel disc wheels featuring Rudge central wheel locks otherwise only available as an option at extra cost.

The aluminum SLs came with *two* complete rear-end assemblies, a standard ratio,

usually 3.64:1 or 3.89:1, and the owner's choice of a second rear axle geared in any of three additional combinations. For hill climbs or short courses a 4.11 ratio was offered, while for higher top speeds and long courses, the recommendation was a 3:42. The greatest maximum speed was achieved by cars fitted with a 3.25:1 ratio. As tested by Daimler-Benz, these cars were capable of 161 mph.

Aside from the aluminum body and plexiglass windows, the alloy coupes were identical to the steel cars on the inside and equipped with the same four-speed synchromesh transmission geared first through fourth at 3.34:1, 1.97:1, 1.39:1, and 1:1.

The difference in price between a steel coupe and alloy SL was less than $1,000 and the total price of an alloy car was under

Ventilation was always a problem with the coupes. Air taken in through the cowl was expelled through the roof vents, which were open to the interior. The angle and design prevented water from entering the car.

Opposite page
A striking combination, the 300SL Gullwing coupe and 300SL roadster in matching Strawberry Red. Both cars also have matching natural leather upholstery. They were restored by Hjeltness Restorations in Escondido, California.

$8,000. Of the twenty-six built in 1955 and the three built in 1956, the locations of all but one are known today.

The majority of the alloy cars were sold to privateers and early owners included John von Neumann, Tony Parravano, Briggs Cunningham, and Ferrari's Luigi Chinetti.

The first aluminum Gullwing coupe was built with chassis number 198 040-55 00173 and body number 198 040-55 00001. After this car was delivered, the 040 designation in the serial number sequence was changed to 043 to distinguish the aluminum-bodied coupes.

This first car was shipped to Mercedes-Benz Distributors, Inc. in New York, on March 31, 1955, order number 681 466 finished in DB 50 White with 1079 Red Leather interior.

The original owner was Carl Kiekhaefer, founder of Mercury Marine, manufacturers of Mercury outboard motors. In the mid-1950s, Kiekhaefer fielded a team of Chrysler 300s that won three consecutive NASCAR championships. The white 300SL only raced once. Driven by Tim Flock for Kiekhaefer's Mercury Marine team, the car qualified for the pole position in a 100-mile sports car endurance race at Raleigh Speedway in North Carolina on August 6, 1955. Flock led the field from the start and was never passed. After the race, Kiekhaefer retired the car.

The aluminum coupes were instrumental in establishing the 300SL's racing history, and later Bonneville speed record. The historic Bonneville run took place in 1967, with world-renowned 300SL collector Don Ricardo setting a record speed of 153.711mph in Class E Grand Touring.

In 1967, Ricardo was already 59 years old, but the indomitable former big band leader had no intention of letting age prevent him from setting a world record. His car

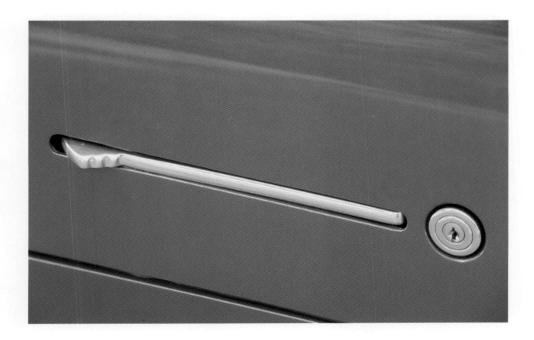

was the sixteenth aluminum coupe built, number 198 043-55 00426, purchased from original owner Bob Frentress. "I restored the car and rebuilt the engine myself for Bonneville," says Ricardo, who also owned the former Tony Parravano alloy coupe.

The most memorable image of Ricardo's assault on the Bonneville record comes from the timer, who believed the car's engine had exploded at the end of his first run. Ricardo recalls the incident twenty-seven years later, with a hint of laughter in his voice. "I was approaching 150 miles per hour when all of a sudden the left door came open. It sounded like a sonic boom, and from a distance it looked as if the hood had come up, that's why everyone thought the engine had blown." Amazingly, Ricardo kept the car going straight, even with the door open and the left side of the coupe momentarily off the ground. He returned to the staging area, tied the door shut, went back out, and set a world record.

Recessed door handle design

was a unique 300SL trait.

Opposite page

No sports car in postwar

automotive history has

become as recognized the

world over as the 300SL

Gullwing coupe. Of the 1,400

examples built, nearly 1,000

are extant. Having become

treasured collectibles, some

of the more rare models are

valued as high as $700,000

today.

With the spare consuming
most of the trunk, there was
little room for cargo except
behind the front seats.

Previous page left
The 300SL became the most
famous automotive design
of the 1950s and one of the
greatest of all time. Considered
a "civilized" version of the
1952 race cars, the Gullwing
coupe was the perfect race car
cum road car.

Previous page right
The elegant, flowing lines of
the 300SL coupe become even
more apparent when viewed
from above. In the words of
designer Karl Wilfert, it was a
true example of "form follows
function."

Opposite page
The 300SL engine was in itself a
work of art and finely detailed
by Daimler-Benz engineers.

Challenged by Jaguars, Austin-Healeys, and other GTs, Ricardo's Bonneville record remained unbroken for more than a decade.

An abstraction of Charles Dickens' famous opening from *A Tale Of Two Cities* best described 300SL ownership: "It was the best of cars, it was the worst of cars...."

Daimler-Benz designers Karl Wilfert and Paul Braiq had done an incredible job of turning a purpose-built race car into a civilized, road-going sports car—and in less than a year's time. Still, underneath Wilfert's streamlined bodywork and luxuriously appointed interior, the 300SL had changed little from the original 1952 competition coupes.

Air conditioning was not available and the only ventilation was through the cowl and small quarter windows in the doors. Entry and exit was over the wide elbow-high doorsill—always a test of one's patience and grace. Luggage was restricted to a bag or two in the trunk and what could be packed in the optional two-piece fitted luggage set. And unless one had exceptional skills, driving the 300SL properly and effectively was no easy task. For every measure of inconvenience, however, there was an equal and opposite measure of irrepressible satisfaction, even in the simple act of opening the doors.

In keeping with the 300SL's aerodynamic shape, there were no protruding door handles. Recessed in the lower section of the door was an aluminum-alloy rod with a small

raised section on one side; all you had to do was press it and the rest of the handle withdrew from the recess. A simple tug on the hand lever and the door unlatched, swinging upward majestically on two chrome-plated spring assisted cylinders.

The task of getting into the car seemed of little consequence once you were settled behind the wheel. In front of you there was a 215hp, fuel-injected engine capable of attaining speeds in excess of 150mph, and in the rear, a capacious 34.3 gallon fuel tank to feed it.

From behind the wheel, the driver had a clear view of the instrument panel. Housed on the left was an 8000rpm tachometer; on the right, a 160mph speedometer. Two warning lights were also located in the upper part of the dashboard—one in blue for the

high beam at the top, one in yellow for the turn indicators further down. Two small gauges were located to the left of the steering wheel for fuel level and oil pressure; to the right, another pair for oil and water temperature. Prominently displayed in the center of the dashboard was a clock in matching style to the gauges. In the lower section of the panel a series of chrome-plated switches to operate the lights, windshield wipers, and heating and ventilation systems were arranged within easy reach of the driver.

The SL's firm bucket seats gave excellent support, while the wide doorsills created a perfect armrest. All-around visibility was excellent, and thanks to the high fenders, drivers found it easy to get a feel for the car's length and width. After a few minutes be-

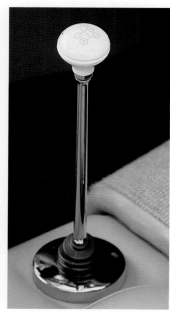

hind the wheel, the 300SL seemed as familiar as a well-worn pair of driving gloves.

Odd as it may sound, back in 1954 when New York importer Max Hoffman took an order for a Mercedes-Benz 300SL, unless the buyer specified color and interior choice—and surprisingly, not everyone did—you received the factory's standard order:

metallic silver gray exterior, blue gaberdine plaid and tex-leather upholstery, blue trim, and blue German weave square carpeting.

The silver and plaid combination were not only tasteful in 1954, but historically significant. Silver is Mercedes' traditional racing color, and gaberdine plaid upholstery something of a Mercedes-Benz tradition.

Plaid was used for the seat upholstery on

In 1956, Prince Metternich finished sixth in the Mille Miglia.

Opposite page

The 300SL was a timeless sports car design.

Among the fastest 300SLs were those fitted with lighter-weight aluminum-alloy bodies and the competition or sports camshaft.

all of the 300SL competition cars in 1952, again on the 1953 fuel-injected 300SL prototype, and for the 1954 300SLR coupes and roadsters. The busy, crosshatched pattern upholstery was also used to cover the seat of Juan Manual Fangio's 1954 and 1955 world championship W196 race cars. The fabric

used on the production 300SL coupes was a great deal more significant than most buyers realized. The same can be said of later 300SL owners, who in almost every instance, have had the cars restored and reupholstered in leather, without any consideration for the plaid interior's tradition.

Mercedes-Benz 300SL

In all, there were three combinations available: blue plaid with blue tex-leather, (tex-leather being a gracious classification for vinyl); green with green tex-leather; and red with creme tex-leather. On coupes produced from 1954 through 1956, leather was available as an option, as was a set of fitted luggage.

For its time, the 300SL coupe was an exemplary design, with a proven four-wheel independent suspension and large, effective drum brakes. The suspension and brakes were trend setters at the time and a comparison with modern Mercedes models merely shows how much progress has been made over the years, although the 300SL certainly proves that Daimler-Benz engineers in the 1950s did a good job.

The clean, simple lines of the 300SL grille have become a Mercedes-Benz trademark and an image recognized the world over.

Right
The powerful M198 fuel-injected six-cylinder engine used in the 300SL delivered 215bhp at 5800rpm. Engines in the alloy-bodied cars were specially equipped with a competition camshaft.

By today's standards, one could say that the 300SL is lacking in almost every important area—handling, braking, comfort, and convenience. Yet there isn't a car built today—not even the brand-new Mercedes-Benz V-12-powered SL600 convertible—that can cast so impressive a shadow as an open 300SL Gullwing door.

Interior upholstery choices were either gaberdine plaid with tex-leather (vinyl), or hand-sewn leather throughout.

The instrument panel was comprised of two large dials: the 8000rpm tachometer on the left and the 160mph speedometer on the right. Two warning lights were also located in the upper part of the dashboard: one for the high beam (blue) at the top, one for the turning indicators (yellow) further down. Two small gauges were located to the left of the steering wheel: fuel gauge and oil pressure. And to the right, another pair: oil and water temperature. A series of chrome-plated switches to operate the lights, windshield wipers, heating, and ventilation were arranged within easy reach of the driver.

The Rudge competition knock-off wheels weighed more, but the weight penalty was offset by the increased speed with which they could be changed.

Race-modified models were equipped with steel disc wheels featuring Rudge central wheel locks otherwise only available as an option at extra cost.

Opposite page
With the 3.25:1 rear axle ratio, alloy-bodied coupes claimed a top speed of 161mph. The cars were also fitted with higher-rated coil springs, stiffer shocks, and Dunlop racing tires.

Opposite page and left

Rare by numbers, only 1,400 Mercedes-Benz 300SL coupes were built, and of those only thirteen were ordered in Strawberry Red and only a few of those with natural leather upholstery. The rarest combination was Strawberry Red with red gaberdine plaid upholstery.

300SLs came equipped with Continental or Englebert tires on 5.50x15 J painted wheels with hubcap. Options were 6.50x15 extra super-sport or 6.50x15 racing tires. Many owners fit their cars with Michelin tires today.

Every corner of the 300SL had a curved surface. There were no hard edges in the design, which contributed to the car's phenomenal drag coefficient. In the 1950s, this was the most aerodynamic production car on the road.

Opposite page

Interiors were straightforward in design. This is the first alloy-bodied 300SL coupe built, delivered to Max Hoffman on March 31, 1955. The upholstery color was listed as 1079 red leather. Hoffman sold the car to sportsman Carl Kiekhaefer, founder of Mercury Marine.

Details of a perfect restoration: The correct operation stickers and well-finished components in the 300SL engine bay.

Elegant details highlighted the dash of the coupe like jewelry.

Opposite page

As a matter of record all 300SL coupes had aluminum doors, trunk lids, hoods, and rocker panels; however, on the alloy-bodied competition cars, the entire body was built of alloy. The engine in the alloy cars came with the competition camshaft and a 240bhp output.

THE 300SL ROADSTER

FROM WINGS TO WIND

The evolution of the 300SL from coupe to roadster, at least as a production car, was far more complicated and costly than the 1952 "conversions" rendered on the 300SL competition cars.

Rarely in automotive history has the introduction of a roadster version precluded production of the coupe upon which it was based. With the 300SL roadster, however, it was indeed a case of succession. While there has always been great speculation as to the reason for the Gullwing's demise, it was the opinion of Heinz Hoppe that in part it was a result of comments made to Daimler-Benz management by Max Hoffman.

"A vast majority of the cars went to the States, and Maxie Hoffman told us time and again that his pampered customers wanted a bit more comfort, a larger boot, and a bit more fresh air. In addition, we didn't know how long customers—who can be pretty choosy in this price range—would accept a car so similar to the racing version with all its compromises. That's why we started considering a roadster offering that extra creature comfort American customers like so much—and the roadster then went into production in 1957."

Whether or not Hoffman prompted the decision, in 1957 the last seventy Gullwings were delivered to customers, and by year's end 618 roadsters had already come off the assembly line.

Opposite page

The 300SL roadster prototype after being restored to its 1956 300SLS configuration.

The roadster was introduced in 1957 at the Geneva Motor Show. Daimler-Benz proudly stated that "the 300 SL Roadster is our response to the demand in many countries for a particularly fast, comfortable, open sports car. This automobile offers a wide range of technical achievements for even greater driving safety and motoring comfort as well as a high standard of practical everyday value for touring in real style."

Contrary to popular belief, planning for the 300SL roadster began before the first production coupes were even delivered. Archive documents indicate that design and construction was to take place beginning in October 1954, with the first roadster prototype being completed for evaluation by top manage-ment in November 1955. The designers of the Gullwing were well aware of its shortcomings from the beginning: no real luggage or trunk area; difficult handling due to the high pivot rear axle; difficult entry and exit due to the high doorsills. The new roadster would solve these problems. Additionally, they felt an open model sports car would prove more popular in places like Southern California where they hoped to sell a lot of the 300SLs.

The story of how the design came about is one of the most interesting in 300SL lore. The history of the SLS prototype is in effect the history of the 300SL roadster. The story actually begins following a one-two finish at Le Mans in June 1952 when four of the original Gullwing prototypes were converted to

Previous page and right

"Accustomed to success":

the 300SL roadster brochure.

Frank Barrett Collection

Opposite page

Collier's *magazine*

photojournalist David Douglas

Duncan was privy to the secret

Design Studio at Daimler-Benz,

where he photographed a

300SL prototype being worked

on. In the foreground, Fritz

Nallinger (center) and Karl

Wilfert (right) discuss the

roadster design.

ACCUSTOMED TO SUCCESS

Only a few automobile models in the world have achieved their maturity through such exhaustive tests as has the 300 SL. From the first prototype entered in many races up to the internationally recognized 300 SL series sports car with its typical gull-winged doors, this famous vehicle has achieved countless successes. Simultaneously, it has had to stand tests which could never be duplicated by stationary test stand methods and only approximately imitated. Specialists, experts and distinctive automobile enthusiasts praise today as then the quality of this vehicle and marvel at many of the details within some of its completely new designing principles. This consecutive development has been crowned by the production of the 300 SL roadster or coupe – a car for everyone who wants to express his delight in sports and speed and his sense of beauty through the ownership of one of the finest thoroughbreds on the market.

Mercedes-Benz 300SL

Chassis 00009/52 bodied as the 300SL roadster prototype, with Nallinger, Uhlenhaut, and Mercedes Experimental Department foreman Edwin Hitzelberger. Picture was taken by photojournalist David Douglas Duncan.

roadsters. Mercedes took off the roofs to lighten the vehicles and also simplified some other components to reduce weight. These sleek converted Gullwings were actually the first 300SL roadsters. One of these cars, 00009/52, became a test vehicle following the 1952 racing season and was fitted with a fuel-injected motor in 1953. With its racing body removed in early 1955, the chassis served as the platform upon which the prototype body for the coming production

roadster was constructed.

The 300SLS prototype first came to the attention of Mercedes restoration expert Scott Grundfor in the early 1980s when a private collector called and told him that he had a 300SL roadster he would like inspected as he was considering restoring it. He mentioned to Grundfor that the car was a prototype but he didn't know its complete history.

Mercedes historian Robert Nitske conducted research concerning the vehicle in the late 1970s during a trip to the archives in Stuttgart. Through the chassis number, Nitske was able to discover that the chassis of this vehicle had originally belonged to an earlier series of Gullwing prototypes, specifically chassis 00009/52 driven by Fritz Reiss in the Nürburgring race. It had also been raced at Le Mans, coming in behind Hermann Lang, with Theo Helfrich and Norbert Niedermayer driving the car to a second-place finish, and finally in the Carrera PanAmericana with driver John Fitch.

Most of the Mercedes-Benz prototype and racing vehicles were retained by the factory and few found their way into private hands. The prospect of having actually discovered one of the factory prototypes intrigued Grundfor. He looked at the car and discussed restoration options with the owner. It had been stripped to bare metal and completely disassembled. No decision was reached at that

The SLS roadster prototype in August 1956, with designer Fritz Nallinger at the wheel as photographed by David Douglas Duncan for Collier's *magazine.*

time and several years passed before the owner decided not to restore the car. In 1987, Grundfor was able to acquire the car and begin the research and restoration.

At that time there was still little information on the prototype regarding its complete history; should the existing roadster body be discarded to recreate the 1952 racer? Was it merely one of several roadster pre-production test vehicles? Grundfor began a period of research that took him to the Mercedes-Benz factory and to their museum in Stuttgart. The director of the archive, Max VonPein, graciously extended the assistance of his staff in the research. Unfortunately, the records on this particular vehicle were sketchy at best. It was explained that records for some of these unusual cars had apparently been misplaced, lost, or had yet to be properly organized.

A period of many months of frustration passed with numerous letters written, but few questions answered. It was beginning to seem a hopeless task. By chance Grundfor recalled one stone that had been left unturned. Among the information the former owner had given him was a note that stated simply, "300SL article - *Collier's* - 1956." When he tracked down *Collier's* magazine of October 12, 1956, he found on page 29 a full color, four-page article that featured the 300SLS prototype. The article gave a name to the vehicle and a rather complete description of what it was. The title of the article was "The Secret SLS" and indicated that this vehicle was the very first 300SL roadster. It included pictures of the car taken by photojournalist David Douglas Duncan.

In the article Duncan detailed his visit to Germany and Switzerland where he photographed the new sports car being tested by designer Karl Wilfert. Duncan wrote, "Though much technical data is still cloaked

Right out of Duncan's
Collier's *article, a German*
Shepherd named Rolf smiles
for the camera, with the
300SL roadster prototype
in the background.

in secrecy, factory officials have released enough details with these exclusive Collier's photos to give a clear idea of what that streaking shape really is when standing still. A giant two seater convertible roadster combining features of Mercedes revolutionary Gullwing doored 300SL Coupe and the streamlined racer in which Juan Manuel Fangio of Argentina beat the world on the Grand Prix circuit, the World Series of professional racing. The SLS Super Light Special clears the ground by a hand and stands but 33 inches high at the door cowling, lower than the ears of the police dogs assigned to guard it. Designed by racing experts for sportsmen to whom the final product is the

only consideration, the 300SLS is unlikely to become the second car in every man's garage. It is meant to be the crown jewel of all sports cars."

Among the pictures were some of the car at the secret design studio of Mercedes-Benz in Stuttgart, which rarely, if ever, had been opened to photographers or to the press.

Duncan told Grundfor Mercedes officials approached him regarding the story when he went to Stuttgart to pick up his own shiny new black Gullwing (which he still drives today). Grundfor was eventually able to acquire all the Collier's photos as well as some earlier archive photos which greatly aided in authenticating the restoration.

Opposite page
Rudolf Uhlenhaut checks
the grille on 300SL roadster
prototype as Fritz Nallinger
(standing) and Edwin
Hitzelberger look on. Picture
was taken by Duncan for
his 1956 Collier's *article.*

As the prototype 300SL

roadster in 1955, 00009/52

was equipped with bumpers,

convertible top, and body trim.

Note the fuel filler door missing

from the left fender.

Changing the 300SL from coupe to convertible had posed some difficult problems for Mercedes-Benz. Convertibles tend to be heavier than their coupe counterparts and increasing weight decreases performance. As performance would be a critical selling point for the 300SL roadster, weight was a big problem. The 1952 Gullwing racing chassis weighed 110lb stripped down as opposed to 181lb for the production Gullwing. Daimler-Benz engineers chose one of these lightweight chassis, number 00009/52, as the platform upon which to build the roadster prototype body. The problem Uhlenhaut's engineers faced was that the tubular spaceframe was far too high to provide room for doors hinged at the front. It would have to be modified to accommodate the roadster's hinged doors without compromising chassis strength.

During the restoration of the SLS, Grund-for could see evidence of how this problem was originally approached. The chassis had been reinforced with gusset plates at the weak points in the lower section of the frame where tubes had been cut away to allow use of a conventional door. However, there was still too much chassis flexing and the tubes had to be reinstalled. From the outside the roadster still had a regular door, but when you opened it, the chassis tubes were sticking through the door jamb so that occupants would have to climb over them to enter or exit the car. This of course, proved unsuccessful.

Another alteration discovered on the roadster prototype was what Daimler-Benz engineers referred to as a "middle tunnel structure" that ran between the seats to reinforce the structural integrity of the chassis, which had been compromised by removing the roof and lowering the frame to accom-

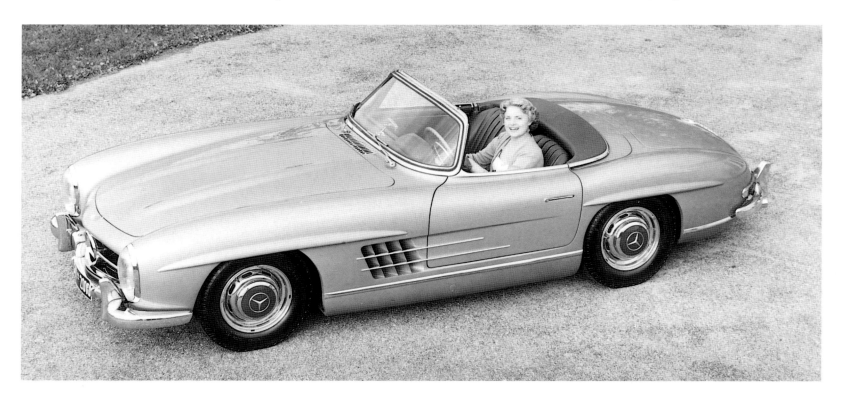

modate conventional doors. This was another stop-gap measure that did not solve the problem. The final solution to the chassis design was to use larger-diameter and much heavier-gauge tubing in order to provide the necessary strength. The frame remained virtually as it was in the 300SL coupe from the firewall forward, and the cross member above the rear axle also remained at the same height; however, from the firewall back the frame became much lower and more compact in order to provide space for the doors and the larger luggage compartment. Unfortunately, this greatly increased the curb weight Uhlenhaut and his staff had worked so hard to minimize. It was nevertheless the only viable solution.

As a prototype car, the SLS combined a variety of features from the 300SL coupe with new ideas that were still being evaluated. For example, the front fenders and grille opening

Rebodied as the 300SLS

prototype, the car was

photographed at Monza in

1956, with race driver Karl

Kling, (leaning in over door)

and the great Alfred Neubauer,

Director of Mercedes-Benz

Racing Department (standing

to the left). You might take

note of all the 356 Porsches

in the background.

*The ultimate erector set,
the chassis for the second
roadster prototype with the
"mid tunnel" tubing in place.*

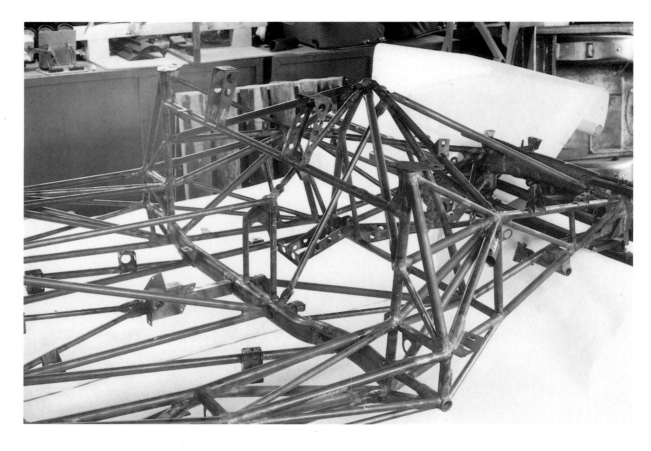

*When the 300SL roadster
prototype was being restored
by Scott Grundfor, he
discovered experimental disc
brakes on the front wheels.*

were far more pronounced, giving the SLS an aggressive, almost Ferrari-like, appearance. The grille design was also unique. Although similar in shape, the trim had a predominant lower lip that projected out over the body, and the concave barrel star in the center was from an early 300SL coupe. The windshield wiper mechanism was a carry-over from the race cars, which aided in identifying the car from early photographs as they park on the "wrong" side of the windshield. The prototype also had bolt-on fender eyebrows that were separated from the body by a welting.

Inside, the dashboard was quite different from that of the production car with a pull-out ashtray, a nice piece, but it proved too complicated for the production car. The pro-

totype had a fiber optic light bar to illuminate the knobs and levers on the lower part of the dash, another good idea but probably too cumbersome for production. The physical design of the dash, the placement of the clock, the mirror, and miscellaneous other items were different on the SLS as well. The steering wheel was unique to this car, having an almost American Futura deep-dish styling look. The transmission was from the race cars and early production coupes, tucked far forward under the dash, and coupled by a

American Paul O'Shea pulls one of the 300SLS roadsters past a D-Type Jaguar in SCCA competition. **Daimler-Benz AG**

Mercedes-Benz 300SL

lengthy shift lever from a 300 sedan.

The body had lightened panels—again in keeping with the concern for holding the weight down—that appeared to be carry overs from the racing vehicle. The trunk and tonneau cover inner-struc-

tures were all drilled out to save weight.

After being completed in 1955, the car, along with several other prototypes, was used for public displays, publicity photographs, sales brochures, and in the *Collier's* article by David Douglas Duncan.

Interior of prototype 300SL roadster featured the revised instrument pod that would be used on production models.

Although Mercedes had officially withdrawn from racing in 1955, Daimler-Benz of North America urged Stuttgart to enter the new roadsters in Sports Car Club of America races for 1957, to help in promoting the car's US introduction.

The roadster prototype was rebodied by Alfred Neubauer's Sports Department. On its third life as the SLS racing prototype, 00009/52 was used to develop the 300SLS competition roadsters shipped to American race driver Paul O'Shea and has perhaps the first set of disk brakes that were ever tested on a Mercedes vehicle. They look similar to Dunlop brakes except they were hand machined and were mounted on the front only. However, since the prototype had the original and less-responsive Gullwing-type swing-axle rear suspension, it

Twin exhausts used on the 1956 300SLS prototype were derived from the 300SLR roadster and coupe designs. The direct exhaust was extraordinarily loud, especially on the roadster. Conversation was virtually impossible in the car!

Opposite page, top and far left
Bumpers and rear exhaust pipe were removed from the roadster prototype when it was used for the SLS and the openings in the body covered with riveted plates. The roadster prototype in SLS configuration had direct exhaust pipes cut through the fender. The same design was used on the two SLS race cars built for the 1957 SCCA season.

Opposite page, left
The 300SL roadster prototype was fitted with the original European-style headlight design, which contained three lighting elements in one large lens configuration.

Sweeping lines of the 300SL roadster were beautifully sculpted by designers Karl Wilfert and Paul Braiq. Note the delicate curves of the decklid and fender and how perfectly they meet, one form flowing into the other. Today, not an uncommon design trait, but in 1957, quite an accomplishment.

Opposite page

The front fenders and grille opening of the SL roadster prototype were far more pronounced, giving it an aggressive, almost Ferrari-like appearance. The grille design was also unique to the prototype roadster. Although similar in shape, the trim had a predominant lower lip that projected out over the body. The concave barrel star in the center was from an early 300SL coupe.

was never raced or shipped to O'Shea.

The first SLS race car was completed on March 29, the second on April 2, 1957. While a lot of the ex-Racing Department's know-how went into the 300SLS, Daimler-Benz did everything to avoid the impression that the two cars for the O'Shea/Tilp team might be works cars, since the Racing Department had been officially closed down at the end of 1955.

Paul O'Shea remembered his days racing the early 300SLs. After he won the American Sports Car Championship in 1956, he had been asked by Uhlenhaut to come to Germany and test drive the new roadster prototype to see if it might be competitive for racing in the 1957 season. In October 1956, he demonstrated the car at the Solitude circuit on the occasion of its unveiling to the international motoring press. He then took the car for testing to the Nürburgring and Hockenheim tracks and based on his tests there, concluded that a lightened car might be competitive in the upcoming Sports Car Series in the United States.

The car, as Grundfor found it, was amazingly complete. The only major piece that was missing from the SLS version was the original wood-rimmed steering wheel. Grundfor was able to locate the original wheel but its owner was unwilling to sell; he did, however, let the restorer copy it.

Grundfor also had a photo that showed Karl Kling and Alfred Neubauer with the SLS at Monza during a rally in late 1956. When

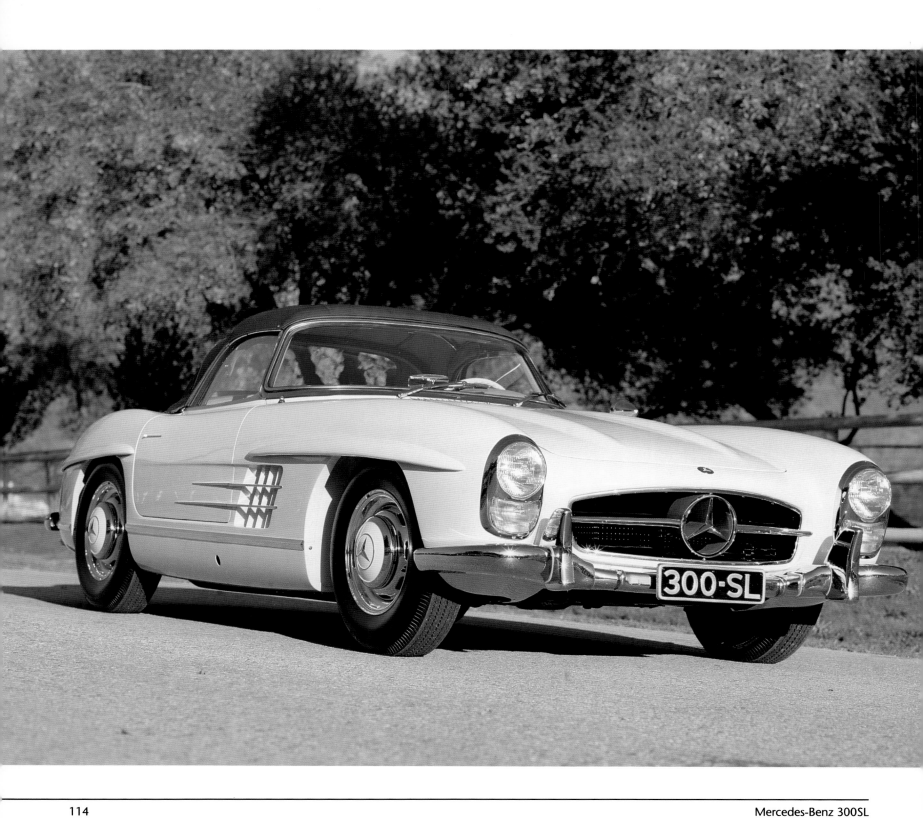

The 300SL roadster introduced a new headlight shape that incorporated a larger two-piece design with a lower lens and stylish chromed bezel. European models of the 300SL roadster were fitted with a one-piece lens that was not exported to the United States.

Opposite page

The production 300SL roadster closely resembled the prototype but had distinctively different lines around the grille. A total of 1,858 roadsters were built between 1957 and 1964.

MERCEDES-BENZ *Type 300 SL*
ROADSTER

1957

TOP GRADE FOR STYLE AND PERFORMANCE

The Daimler-Benz AG is now introducing you to the racy, elegant brother of the swiftest and strongest German production sports-car. It is the Type 300 SL Roadster. The dynamic outline of its sprawling body denotes the powerful energy which this car can instantly unleash at your command. Although the impressive performance of its 250 HP six cylinder short-stroke engine with gasoline injection gives the 300 SL Roadster a race-track character, this vehicle can be steered without trouble at walking pace through dense city traffic. By its insensitivity, its manoeuvrability, its excellent road holding and its appointments it is a sports and a touring car to exactly the same degree. Whether you choose the standard version of the Roadster or the de luxe version, with bumpers and additional interior appointments, the Type 300 SL Roadster is always ready to prove its high spirits when and where you like. In sporting use and in luxurious travelling for fast, comfort discerning drivers this fascinating car, with the style of the automobiles of the future, offers you technical novelties, appointments and safety — everything which you can expect from a modern vehicle.

Roadster with bumpers, closed

Roadster without bumpers, open

the car was used for pictures in that year, it was fitted with what were to become the production-style bumpers and chromed speed lines. Redone as the O'Shea prototype the following year, the bumpers and trim were removed and never replaced. The openings for both the front and rear bumper mounts were covered by riveted plates, as they are today. The exhaust was also altered,

ducted through two short, unmuffled pipes exiting from the right front rocker panel, just aft of the air vents. This was the way in which the SLS has been restored.

The prototype had been used as a design and styling exercise so that the engineers and stylists at Mercedes-Benz could put into actual physical shape the ideas they had re-

Mercedes-Benz sales flyer 1957.

Frank Barrett Collection

Opposite page

The 300SL roadster became

more than the Gullwing coupe.

After the coupe top has been fitted into the pins for the roadster top cover, it is easily lowered and secured by the tommy locks.

Ventilation has been particularly well designed for the coupe. The ventilation intake slits for supplementary fresh air are located directly in front of the windshield.

The outflowing air slits are located in the upper rear edge of the wide, overslung roof. In this way the interior is ventilated without draft even during fast driving or hot weather.

The personal elegance of the coupe is emphasized by the wide panorama rear window sweeping toward the front. This allows, in conjunction with the panorama windshield and two windows which roll all the way down, an all-round view seldom so perfect in sports coupes. The bright plastic lined roof gives the coupe a groomed atmosphere. The coupe is quickly transformed into a thoroughbred roadster again — the top can be easily removed by two persons and replaced by the roadster top. Moreover, the roadster top can remain in the car even when using the coupe hard top if one doesn't need to use the large space back of the seats for luggage. This striking coupe top is available for all 300 SL roadsters delivered to date so that the owners can transform their cars into elegant coupes.

Six cylinder high performance engine with direct gasoline injection, output of 240 HP/6100 r.p.m. and 250 HP/6200 r.p.m. depending on compression, maximum speed depending on equipment aprox. 155 m/h, fuel consumption according to driving manner, 12 to 19 lit/100 km (23.5—14.9 m.p. Imp. gal; 19.6—12.4 m.p. U.S. gal), tank capacity, 100 lit. (22/26 Imp./U.S. gal), pay load, 230 kg (505 lbs).

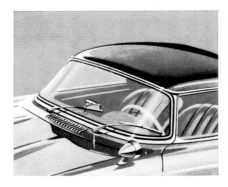 

Printed in Germany **310** 1058 e

Mercedes-Benz sales flyer from 1959 showing the virtues of the roadster softtop and hardtop.
Frank Barrett Collection

garding the new project. They could look at it, and test it, and touch it, and if necessary, change it. During the restoration of the car Grundfor found many things that had been modified and changed. For example, the fuel tank filler started on one side of the car and then it was moved to the other side; the dashboard underwent numerous revisions as did the chassis; originally the real flooring of the

car had supported the Gullwing chassis with twin spares; this was changed and modified numerous times; however, the floorpans from the original racer still appear to be in the car.

Constructed to assess public reaction to the new design, it was the only roadster that existed in this 300SL series for almost a year, until 1956 when Mercedes-Benz built a second and then third prototype. It was

10. Tommy handle for engine hood lock. See p. 10 for opening and closing of the engine hood.

11. Control lever for the overtaking signal light. This is combined with a horn. If it is pushed back beyond a stop, the horn is actuated in addition to the overtaking signal light.

12. Ventilation and heating levers for the left side of the car (see p. 11).

13. Ventilation and heating levers for the right side of the car (see p. 11).

14. Electric clock: this is set by depressing and turning the knob at the clock.

15. Lockable glove compartment; when the lid is opened, it is illuminated by an interior light.

16. Electric cigarette lighter: press the button for a few seconds until the heating coil glows red.

17. Ash tray. To empty it, pull out the ash tray; the lower part can be removed by pressing on the sides.

18. Rear view mirror. Fold back the control lever to bring it into anti-glare position.

19. Speedometer with total and trip mileage recorder (see page 9).

20. Combi-instrument (see p. 10).

21. Tachometer.

22. Cushion-mounted sun visor (1 each on the right and left side). The sun visor is only supplied upon special request.

23. Light of interior department; is also used as courtesy light. A screen over the light serves to switch on and over:
Screen closed: light is switched off.
Screen half-opened: courtesy light. When the driver's door is opened, the light is switched on by a door contact switch and remains lighted as long as the driver's door is opened.
Screen completely opened: map light; light burns constantly.
When you get out of the car, you should always set the screen to the "courtesy light" position.
The seats can be adjusted backwards and forwards.
Depress the lever at the seat, shift the seat backwards or forwards, and let the lever go.

Driver's seat

1. Foot dimmer switch: push down to switch from "dim" to "bright" and vice-versa. The blue warning lamp at the lower part of the combi-instrument (see p. 10) lights up when the bright light is switched on.

2. Clutch pedal.

3. Brake pedal.

4. Accelerator pedal.

5. Hand brake lever.

6. Gear shift lever; 4 forward speeds, fully-synchronized, 1 reverse gear (see p. 18).

7. Tommy handle to actuate the supplementary ventilation (see p. 11).

8. Contact ring for horn and blinkers: push down to actuate the horn. Turn to the right or left to switch on the corresponding blinkers. The red warning lamp in the combi-instrument remains lighted as long as the blinkers are switched on.
The contact ring only functions when the ignition is switched on.

9. Control knob for the windshield washing system and wipers. Pushing down to a stop switches on the windshield wipers. Pushing down beyond this stop actuates the windshield washing system. If you push back to the stop, the windshield wipers which now operate alone will dry the windshield. See page 30 for agents to fill into the windshield washing system.

The back rests can be pushed forward; moreover, they can be adjusted in an oblique direction.

Take out the cushion, push the back rest forward, pull out the two retaining bolts below at the back of the seat frame and insert into the next bore required (3 positions). Both bolts should be adjusted to the same degree.

If the seats are upholstered in leather, the upholstery is fitted with longitudinal air grooves and small holes (ventilated seats).

extensively photographed for use in brochures and promotional material as well as by the motoring press. Although rarely identified as a prototype car, it appeared in early promotional literature and is identifiable by looking for its little peculiarities.

Fortunately, this car had never undergone a thorough restoration and so there were many samples of the original materials still with it, especially the upholstery and paint. Parts of the dashboard underneath the leather still retained some of the original metallic blue paint. From this Grundfor was able to match the exterior body color. Also, he was able to

Explanation of the multitude of driver's controls in the roadster as shown in the owners manual.

Daimler-Benz AG

The roadster and roadster coupe offered the best of both worlds and established a Mercedes-Benz SL tradition carried on to this day.

find parts of the original interior still inside the car and was able to take a sample of the original blue leather and duplicate it.

The prototype roadster was kept by Daimler-Benz until 1965. Originally equipped with the M194 carbureted engine in 1952, the factory refitted the roadster with the fuel-injected M198 motor in 1953. The factory sold the car to Karl Jurgen Britsche of Hamburg, Germany, in 1965. Paperwork with the

car stated: "The 300SL roadster was a continuation of the Type SL coupe and had the same designation 300 sports light roadster. This was a prototype car."

Some years later, Britsche sold the SLS to Arthur von Windheim, also of Hamburg. In 1980, American collector and auto dealer Lloyd Ikerd purchased the SLS and brought it back to the United States.

Aside from O'Shea and a few privateers,

The roadster received a completely new instrument panel design and the hand brake was repositioned to the driver's right.

The trunk was a roadster owner's only luggage space, and cars were offered with two leather-upholstered suit cases made to fit the shape of the trunk.

the production 300SL roadsters hardly appeared on the racetrack. The production cars were more popular among celebrities like Clark Gable, Glenn Ford, and Elvis Presley.

Though not as competitive as the coupes, the roadster was the more comfortable and practical of the two 300SL models. The convertible top folded easily and conveniently beneath a hard tonneau that fit flush with the body. A removable hardtop was also available as an option to give the car a more distinctive look and an extra bit of protection in winter.

Beginning in 1961, the roadster was fitted with Dunlop disc brakes, bringing the final evolution of the 300SL to a conclusion. As for the two 300SLS roadsters raced by O'Shea, they never returned to Germany and instead were reportedly sold in the United States. One of the them was priced at

Mercedes-Benz 300SL

The roadster, introduced in 1957, eliminated both the problem with headroom and ventilation in the 300SL.

Opposite page
The 1957 300SL roadster was a more popular car among Americans, who would find open-air motoring more to their liking than the confined cabin of the 300SL coupe. The sweeping lines of the SL convertible captured the look of the 1952 Nürburgring roadsters, conveying the same race-bred design as the production coupes had in 1954.

Removable hardtop gave the roadster a unique appearance and offered better visibility.

$5,000, the other at $6,000. Both cars completely vanished and have not reappeared to this day. All that remains of the SLS is the 00009/52 prototype, and of course, the 1,858 roadsters that descended from it.

When the Gullwing was replaced by the roadster, Mercedes-Benz offered an optional removable hardtop that allowed owners to create a coupe version of the car. With the hardtop, the 300SL took on a look all its own, distinctively different from the Gullwing and roadster.

The 300SL could be ordered with the hardtop and was described in sales literature as the 300SL coupe. "The personal elegance of the coupe is emphasized by the wide panorama window sweeping toward the front."

Mercedes-Benz 300SL

The evolution of a design: the 300SL Gullwing coupe, 300SL roadster, and 300SL roadster coupe. A striking contrast in designs, the cars were very much alike, yet distinctively set apart from one another. The roadster with hardtop made an interesting transition between coupe and convertible. The removable top was available for any roadster.

Opposite page

A striking contrast in design, the coupe and roadster, pictured in the rare Strawberry Red color combination, were a virtual evolution of the 1952 race cars. Among significant changes made from coupe to roadster, was the lengthening of the chrome sweep lines over the fender louvers. On the roadster they extend through the front half of the doors as does a prominent crease line tracing back from the top of the louver box.

THE 300SLR

THE FORMULA FOR RACING

When Daimler-Benz withdrew from racing at the end of its victorious 1952 season, the factory had set its sights on a new series of race cars for the 1954 season; the W196 Formula 1 *monoposto* and its derivatives, the W196 Streamliner and 300SLR roadster. It was a foregone conclusion that the new Formula 1 car could not be developed in time for the 1953 season, and since Daimler-Benz had nothing more to prove with the 300SL, a one season hiatus from racing seemed an appropriate course.

The new 2.5 liter Formula 1 cars raced for the first time at Reims-Gueux in the 1954 French Grand Prix. Considerably different from the straight six that had powered the

First of the Formula 1 cars, the W196 monoposto.

Opposite page
The 300SLR, of which only two were built.

300SL, the M196 engine used in the *monoposto* was a 2496cc straight eight with Bosch direct fuel injection. The M196 was designed with a central crankshaft drive providing a power take-off from the center of the engine (four cylinders in front, four behind). This design significantly reduced torsional vibration and placed the strain of only four cylinders upon the crankshaft. The output was originally 257bhp at 8250rpm, later increased to 280bhp at 8700rpm, with a maximum torque of 182lb-ft at 6300rpm.

In all, ten W196 Grand Prix cars were built, divided between the 1,433lb *monoposto* and the 1,544lb Reims-type streamliners with sleek, aerodynamic alloy bodies. Five of these cars are in the Daimler-Benz Museum today, and one each in the Turin Car Museum in Italy, the Beaulieu Car Museum in England, the Indianapolis Speedway Museum, and the Technical Museum in Vienna. The tenth car was written off as a total loss after a shunt on the factory test track in 1959.

In the 1954 and 1955 seasons, the W196

The Streamliners were truly formidable race cars, with sleek, lightweight aluminum-alloy bodies. The single-seat W196 models were powered by the new M196 engine.

A study in mastering wind resistance, the W196 Streamliners had a decided advantage over many of their less-aerodynamic competitors.

models won a total of eleven out of fourteen races, with Juan Manuel Fangio collecting two world championships in the doing.

The 300SLR sport version arrived in the Spring of 1955, utilizing the same platform as the W196, with an engine enlarged

to 3.0 liters in displacement. The 300SLR roadsters were built specifically to compete in the 1955 World Championship of Makes and in order to conform to Fédération Internationale de l'Automobile specifications for sports cars, the W196 chassis was fitted with a body similar in design to the

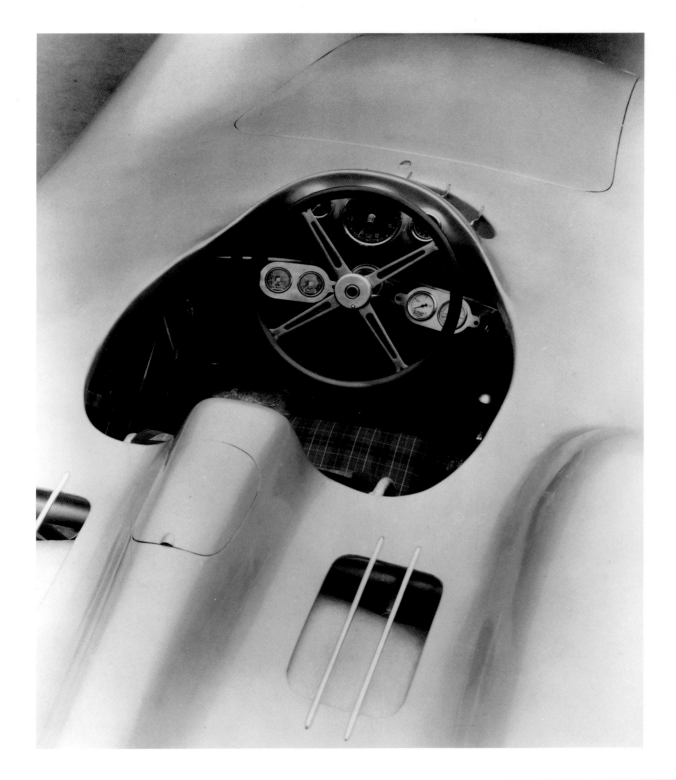

*Cockpit of the W196
Streamliner was gracefully
styled to match the exterior
lines of the car.*

300SL roadsters first seen in 1952.

The SLR's technical features remained virtually unchanged from the *monoposto* and Streamliner, however, since engine size in the World Championship of Makes was limited to 3.0 liters, the capacity of each cylinder was increased from 312 to 374cc, changing the overall displacement from 2496cc to 2992cc. The engine block was also modified for the SLR. The W196 power unit had been welded together out of steel plate, while the SLR featured a light-alloy engine block with a large amount of magnesium. Maximum engine speed was reduced to 7600rpm and the compression ratio was 12.0:1.

Depending upon the race, engine output varied from 276bhp at Le Mans to 302bhp in the Swedish Grand Prix and was reported to be as high as 345bhp, an almost unbelievable rating of nearly 2hp per cubic inch. (Cubic inch displacement for the M196 S engine was 181.9ci).

In conjunction with the aerodynamic bodywork, the 3.0 liter engine was capable of propelling the SLRs to a top speed in excess of 185mph, superbly countered when necessary by the car's massive inboard brakes and innovative hydraulic airbrake, a refinement of the experimental design tested at Le Mans in 1952. The original plan for the SLR had been to build Gullwing-door bodies for the W196S ("S" denoting the sport version) chassis but the drivers who were selected by Alfred Neubauer to drive for the team showed a preference for open cockpit cars, according to journalist Denis Jenkinson, who co-drove the 1955 Mille Miglia with Stirling Moss. Wrote Jenkinson, "It would have been difficult to find a more successful sports/racing car and certainly one so advanced technically." The Moss/Jenkinson car averaged 97.95mph in the Mille Miglia, not only winning but breaking every established record for the 1,000-mile race.

One of the most remarkable features of the SLR was the airbrake, a large flap measuring the width of the

rear cowl and containing the driver's head fairing. When the airbrake was deployed, the downward load it imposed was arranged to pass through the center of gravity of the car, and as well as provide additional braking, it also increased the adhesion of the tires due to the downward pressure exerted.

The two hydraulic arms that raised the airbrake were energized by a pump driven off the gearbox. A lever operated by the driver opened a valve elevating the flap. The original idea behind the airbrake was principally to assist the wheel brakes at the end of the long Mulsanne Straight at Le Mans,

Fitted with a double head fairing, a 300SLR is shown in full competition form.
Daimler-Benz AG

The masters of the road in 1954: Hermann Lang (left), Alfred Neubauer, Juan Manuel Fangio (seated on fender), Karl Kling, and Hans Herrmann.

where heavy braking from 180mph was needed. At the end of the straight, the Mulsanne corner was taken in second gear and a linkage was fitted to the gear-lever mechanism so that when second was selected by the driver the airbrake was automatically lowered. However, Moss discovered he could use it for most corners and save the wheel brakes. He could also corner better at some points by putting the airbrake half way up, thus increasing the load on the tires. As a result, the SLRs were modified so that the airbrake could be operated completely by the driver. Moss, who had one of his best seasons ever behind the wheel of an SLR, said of the airbrake, "It feels as if a giant hand had reached down and grabbed the car by the rear end."

Like the 300SL of 1952, the 300SLRs were virtually unbeatable. Entering seven races in the 1955 season, they crossed the finish line victorious in all but one. The single loss came at Le Mans.

In the 1955 24 Heures du Mans, long-time rivals Mercedes-Benz and Jaguar would face each other once again. Both were counting on their latest cars to win the race. In terms of power and speed, the improved D-Type Jaguars and Mercedes' new 300SLR were equally matched. Both cars had the staying power and the race would be decided by the drivers. Mercedes' hopes were pinned on Fangio, Jaguar's on Mike Hawthorne. It was to be an ill-fated race that would end in tragedy.

For the first time, different classes of cars were competing together at Le Mans. Fangio

Three SLRs lead the field at the 1955 Eifel races. The winners were Fangio, Moss, and Kling.

Upon the personal request of Commendatore Vincenzo Florio, Daimler-Benz entered the 1955 Targa Florio race with the 300SLR. Stirling Moss, whose car was badly damaged, nevertheless won the race at an average speed of 88.4mph.

In what has become the greatest race in the history of the Mille Miglia, Stirling Moss (second from right) and co-driver Denis Jenkinson (center), averaged 97.95mph, not only winning but breaking every established record for the 1,000-mile race. To Jenkinson's immediate right is Daimler-Benz Chief Engineer Rudolf Uhlenhaut. Wrote Jenkinson of the 300SLR, "It would have been difficult to find a more successful sports/racing car and certainly one so advanced technically."

and Hawthorne were the fastest group, and as they battled it out, they had to pass less-powerful cars. It was here that the foundation for disaster had been laid. At 6:30pm, Hawthorne was approaching the pits when he overtook one of the slower cars, an Austin-Healey driven by Lance Macklin. As Hawthorne passed, Pierre Levegh, driving one of the 300SLRs, came up right behind him. Macklin later recalled that Hawthorne's Jaguar passed and then pulled across in front of his Healey. "To my amazement," said Macklin, "his brake lights came on and I swerved to avoid him." All of this in an instant. Macklin had inadvertently cut off Levegh just as he was accelerating, and the 300SLR hit the Austin-Healey square in the backside. Macklin said he could feel the heat of the Mercedes' exhaust as the SLR came around, careening off the rear of the small roadster and into the barrier wall. The Mercedes caught fire on impact, Levegh was killed, and parts of the burning 300SLR were

flung into the crowd taking the lives of more than eighty spectators. It was the worst accident in the history of motor racing.

Eight hours after the fatal collision a telegram was delivered to Neubauer at the pits. In the hours since, the Moss/Fangio and Kling/Salmon 300SLRs had secured first and third places, respectively. The telegram was from Fritz Nallinger in Untertürkheim: "The pride of designers and drivers must bow to the grief suffered by countless French families in this appalling disaster." As a token of their "respect for the dead" the remaining two cars were withdrawn from the race, Hawthorne going on to win a sad and hollow victory for Jaguar.

While Daimler-Benz management had actually planned to withdraw from motor racing immediately after the Le Mans disaster, Neubauer had been able to convince the Board that Mercedes should at least win the title before resigning from the racing scene.

Winning the Mille Miglia on May 1 with Moss and Jenkinson, the International Eifel Race on May 29 and the Swedish Grand Prix on August 1 (in both cases with Juan Manuel Fangio at the wheel), the Tourist Trophy on September 17 (Stirling Moss with John Fitch), and the battle for the Targa Florio on October 16 (Stirling Moss and Peter Collins), the 300SLR clinched the 1955 World Championship of Makes far ahead of its competitors. Moss and Fangio were without question the world's best drivers in 1955 and Mercedes-Benz, builder of the world's best race cars.

In addition to the works race cars, another pair of 300SLRs were built for the 1955 season, but never campaigned. Known as the Uhlenhaut cars, the two additional 300SLR sports racers were fitted with coachwork similar to the 300SL Gullwing coupes, and were actually even better looking. The cars had a long, sleek hood with aerodynamic headlight covers, ex-

72672

British motor journalist Gordon Wilkins was one of the privileged few allowed to test drive the 300SLR coupe. Clocking a top speed of 180mph over the flying kilometer, and 0–100mph in 13.6 seconds, Wilkins found the SLR's braking ability equally impressive: "The unerring wheel grip, and those enormous chassis-mounted inboard brakes produced results that have never before been recorded so far as I am aware."

tra-large air vents in the front fenders, large dual exhaust pipes leading straight out in front of the passenger-side door, (this design was also used on the 300SLR roadsters and would appear again on the 300SLS roadsters in 1957), and a long, sweeping rear deck accented by small, delicate taillights. It was as if the body of a 300SL coupe had been warmed and gently stretched and smoothed in one's hands, with all of the hard edges blended away. Inside, the driving compartment was even smaller than the SL's, and the Gullwing doors more finely sculptured into the fenders. The cockpit was devoid of even the small side windows, the doors nearly meeting the rear wheel arch and curved backlight. It was the 300SL in its purest, albeit most impractical, form.

Chassis numbers 0007/55 and 0008/55, both of which now belong to the Daimler-Benz Museum, were equipped with the W196 302bhp straight eight. Recorded in Jürgen Lewandowski's book, *300 SL Art & Car Edition*, is British motor journalist Gordon Wilkins' comments on the 300SLR coupe. One of the privileged few allowed to drive Uhlenhaut's personal car, he wrote: "I briefly pressed the starter button and the engine roared to life. The noise was mind-boggling, a mixture of valves hammering away, the injection pump purring and gears whining. The closed compartment added the final touch, amplifying all these sounds to an indescribable level. We simply had to use earplugs, which reduced the noise but prevented any kind of conversation. For the purpose of our road test the car had been fitted with an extra-large exhaust silencer intended to lower the noise level to more or less legal standard at least for passers-by (and, of course, for the police)."

The greatest racing driver of all time: Juan Manuel Fangio. In 1991, the Monterey Historic Races paid tribute to the legendary Fangio, pictured here with the W196 monoposto.

Wilkins actually spent several days testing the 300SLR at Monza, on the autobahn and in the Alps, recording more than 2,000 miles behind the wheel. Together with *Automobile Review* of Switzerland editor Robert Braunschweig, Wilkins clocked some extraordinary times in the SLR: a top speed of 180mph over the flying kilometer, 0–50mph in 5.2 seconds, and 0–100mph from a stand in 13.6. Equally impressive was the car's ability to stop. Wrote Wilkins, "The unerring wheel grip, and those enormous chassis-mounted inboard brakes at front and rear, produced braking results that have never before been recorded so far as I am aware." As almost everyone who ever rode in the 300SLR with Uhlenhaut attested, it was an extraordinary car.

The two 300SLR coupes were designed at the same time as the competition roadsters and were at one point being considered for the 1955 Le Mans campaign. Writes Lewandowski: "To this day there are rumors at Daimler-Benz that the Uhlenhaut coupe was to be raced in the fourth Carrera PanAmericana, since coupes with their closed compartment were considered more suitable for an endurance event of that kind. But there never was a fourth Carrera PanAmericana, as the wild romp through Mexico was discontinued once and for all."

Never raced, the coupes were used almost exclusively by Uhlenhaut, who, according to Stirling Moss, would always arrive at races driving one of the 300SLRs. You can imagine the effect this must have had on Mercedes' competitors.

At Laguna Seca Raceway, Fangio, at age 80 in 1991, drives his championship W196 monoposto around the track to a standing ovation of spectators.

Out of the ten SLR roadsters built in the W196S series, eight are still extant. Chassis number 0006/55 was completely destroyed in the Le Mans accident and 0009/55 was never completed. Five of these eight cars still belong to Daimler-Benz as do both of the SLR coupes. Apart from the coupes, chassis number 0002/55 (open with air brake), 0004/55 (open/normal), and 00010/55 (open and extra light) can be found at the Mercedes-Benz Museum. The other models are on display at the Ford Museum in Dearborn, Michigan; the Deutsches Museum in Munich; and the Musé National de l'Automobile in Mulhouse, France.

The W196 Streamliner driven by Fangio to one of his five World Driving Championships, was displayed at Laguna Seca in August 1991.

The powerful M196 Streamliner straight eight engine and massive inboard brakes (large drums behind radiator). Displacing 2496cc, the engine utilized Bosch direct fuel-injection, developing 280bhp at 8700rpm and a maximum torque of 182lb-ft at 6300rpm.

Mercedes-Benz 300SL

Dashboard of the W196 Streamliner was simple and straightforward. The single most important gauge was the center-mounted tachometer.

Interior of the W196 monoposto. Note the traditional gaberdine plaid upholstery.

67 754

A 300SLR roadster with the airbrake deployed. The device, which operated on two hydraulic arms, could be raised and lowered by the driver allowing the cars to rapidly decelerate before going into a corner. Wrote driver Stirling Moss, "It feels as if a giant hand had reached down and grabbed the car by the rear end." Daimler-Benz AG

Mercedes-Benz 300SL

THE RESTORERS

REVERSING THE AGING PROCESS

The wear and tear of time always takes its toll on automobiles, even those that have been carefully stored, because the sustained garaging of an automobile left undriven over any length of time brings on the process of aging and wear in and of itself. The only way to reverse this condition is through restoration, the long and always costly process of remanufacturing an automobile from the ground up. Almost every 300SL you see on the road has been professionally restored, and setting aside the value of the cars in original condition, the cost of restoration has become the single greatest contributing factor to their exorbitantly high market price today.

Throughout the world there are but a handful of restorers who specialize in 300SLs, and given the complexity of these cars, only a specialist should be entrusted with the task of returning an aged 300SL to its former glory.

Hjeltness Restorations, located just outside San Diego, in Escondido, California, has been specializing in 300SL restorations and maintenance since the early 1980s. Owner Jerry Hjeltness, however, has been involved with 300SLs for nearly thirty-five years, since he purchased his first one in 1960.

Hjeltness built a reputation in the 1970s as a specialist in restoring and detailing 300SL engines, and later expanded into the complete restoration of the cars. As he explains, this is one of the most complicated automobiles ever built, and one of the most difficult and challenging to restore.

Over the past decade, Hjeltness has done twenty-three complete body-off restorations, making him one of the world's leading authorities on the construction (and reconstruction) of 300SLs. Explains Hjeltness, "Authenticity is the most important consideration when restoring a 300SL. Throughout the car's production history numerous changes and upgrades were made by Daimler-Benz engineers, and in order to correctly restore a 300SL you must know what was correct for that specific car when it was originally built." Hjeltness adds that many times previous owners have made changes to their car or made repairs with parts from later models. Then too, older restorations may not have been carefully researched. There are countless pitfalls, which can range from the obvious, such as the wrong grille on an early

Throughout the world there are but a handful of restorers who specialize in 300SLs. Hjeltness Restorations, located in Escondido, California, is exemplary of the firms that return these cars to like-new condition. Hjeltness has completed twenty-three frame-off restorations over the last ten years. The cost of a frame-off restoration in 1994 is still comparable to a nice house in most parts of the country: roughly $200,000. The result is a like-new car, ready to take to the road despite being forty years old.

coupe, down to such intricate details as the incorrect plating on bolts.

Oddly enough, one of the biggest problems with 300SLs is over restoration. Notes Hjeltness, "Owners are often unaware of which parts were painted and which were chromed or cad plated, for example, and too much chrome in the engine compartment is just as bad as too little." The 300SL engine was fitted with a unique combination of bolts, washers, nuts, and tubing that varied in finish by virtue of application. As eclectic as that may sound, Mercedes-Benz engineers and designers were specific about these things. "The differences between a car built in 1954 and one built in 1956 are remarkable," says Hjeltness.

The spaceframe is the backbone of the 300SL and without it the body is extremely

Improperly removed from the spaceframe, a 300SL body can suffer extensive damage resulting in misaligned panels. Specially constructed fixtures are used to raise the body from the chassis and other jigs are used during restoration ensuring that the body is held in exactly the same position as it was on the frame.

Reproduction parts must be done authentically: decals, labels, and imprints need to be reproduced for various parts in the engine compartment.

flexible. Improperly removed from the frame, a Gullwing body can suffer extensive damage resulting in misaligned panels. Hjeltness and restorers who specialize in 300SLs have specially constructed fixtures used to raise the body from the chassis, and others in which to place it during restoration, so that the body is held in exactly the same position as it was on the frame. "These fixtures ensure that we can get the door gaps and other panels precisely aligned throughout the restoration process," explains Hjeltness. "Even cars like the 300SL, despite the exacting tolerances built into them, occasionally vary because they were practically hand built. Then too, the fit of aluminum parts, such as the hood and decklid are influenced by the rubber seals used."

*Interiors demand exacting
attention to detail. Upholstery
must be correct for the year
of the car. For example, on
this model perforated leather
was used for the pleats and
the valleys in between. On
an earlier model, perforations
would have only been found
in between the pleats.*

Opposite page

*A complete restoration
demands that every part of
the car be refinished: every
bolt, nut, screw, and washer—
literally thousands of parts in
addition to the body, engine,
suspension, frame and interior.*

Instruments are no longer available for the 300SL, so each gauge must be completely disassembled, refinished, and put back together.

Another costly item for restoration is the disc brakes used on the last 300SL roadsters. If a car has been in storage too long or not driven often enough, the brake cylinders start to leak. Replacement cylinders are no longer available, so they have to be repaired and re-sealed.

The one problem every restorer faces is the availability of replacement parts for the 300SL. Explains Hjeltness, "Seals are no longer available for the injection pumps—the R 3 pump on the Gullwing and the R 8 on the roadster. And when the pump housing itself goes, there's no replacement. That means making a new housing. Brake cylinders are no longer obtainable for the disc brakes introduced on the roadster. There are no replacements for the dash instruments either—so they must be rebuilt and new fascias produced. There are absolutely no wheel rims left with the outer ring made of aluminum, the inner ring of steel. Various body parts are not procurable either, and body panels such as fenders, when damaged beyond repair, have to be handmade over a wooden body buck."

The instrument panel in the 300SL coupe was somewhat less complicated than the roadster's design, however, original gauges are scarce today and reproductions are not totally authentic. A proper restoration demands a labor intensive refurbishing of the original pieces.

Fortunately there are people currently re-producing some of the essential components needed for restoring a 300SL, such as the belly pan. The 300SL coupe has a complete, louvered belly pan underneath the chassis. Rocker panels for both the coupe and road-ster are also available today. Reproduction parts must be done authentically cautions Hjeltness, who goes so far as to have original decals, labels, and imprints reproduced for various parts in the engine compartment, so that every piece under the hood is exactly as it was when new.

Refinishing of gauge fascias and trim is an arduous task demanding the skills of a watchmaker. Leather and metal trim must fit precisely and the instrument panel must be painted to match the car's exterior color.

While the prices of cars may have come down since 1988 and `89, when 300SLs peaked in value, the cost of a frame-off restoration in 1994 is still comparable to a nice house in most parts of the country, roughly $200,000. Why so much? According to Hjeltness, the time spent in rebuilding a car authentically, or to be more precise, "re-manufacturing it" to the same standards as Mercedes-Benz, can run well over 1,000 man hours. In addition there is the often prohibitive cost of parts—a curved star grille can cost up to $10,000; a taillight lens averages $435; even something as rudimentary as the universal slip joint in the roadster rear axle can run more than $6,000.

"While the costs of doing the mechanical work are relatively fixed," says Hjeltness,

Previous page and left
*The early long-neck shifter
was supplied with the first fifty
production coupes—an early
Strawberry Red example under
restoration is pictured—and
also on the prototype 300SL
roadster, which utilized a
coupe driveline.*

Having the grille restored is one of the more costly aspects of a 300SL restoration: the complete assembly can run as much as $10,000. The later designs with straight star and barrel are more common today as some pieces are remanufactured. Original curved star and barrel insets are the most costly since there are no reproduction parts available.

Opposite page

Engine detailing is an art unto itself and restoration shops must ensure that every part is properly painted, coated, or plated. Often, restoration shops and owners over-restore an engine by polishing or chroming too many components. While the end result is perhaps a more dazzling engine compartment, it is nevertheless incorrect.

"when you get into the body, there is no telling what will have to be done until you see what is under the paint." And paint is another costly item. On the average, paint for a 300SL coupe can run $35,000.

A Hjeltness restoration demands that every part of the car be refinished, every bolt, nut, screw, and washer—literally thousands of parts in addition to the body, engine, suspension, frame, and interior. "A quality restoration includes every part of the car, both seen and unseen," says Hjeltness.

Mileage, accidents, and wear are not the only conditions that put 300SLs on the road to the restorer's door. Ironically, the cars sustain a great deal of damage and deterioration from inactivity.

Klaus Kienle, one of Germany's leading 300SL specialists, spent twenty years with Daimler-Benz. "Even today," writes Kienle in Jürgen Lewandowski's book, "the car is still perfect for everyday motoring. And when we do get a car with engine damage, it's usually one that's been standing around too long. The 300SL simply has to be driven—and if the oil temperature is right, it also has to be revved up to the red line from time to time. If it isn't driven often enough, the oil may easily be diluted because it was impossible back then to seal the injection pump perfectly. That means that fuel will get into the oil system and some time or other the film of lubricant will tear open. The result is bearing damage that will cost about $14,000 to re-

pair—provided, that is, that the engine block hasn't been damaged, too." Adds Hjeltness, "The same problem arises with the brakes if the cars are left sitting for too long. Brake fluid collects moisture from the air and a car left sitting can end up with the brake pistons rusted in place. The disc brakes used on the last series of 300SL roadsters also present quite a problem. If a car has been in storage too long or not driven often enough, the brake cylinders start to leak. Replacement cylinders are no longer available, so we have to repair and re-seal the old parts. And that's expensive." Further proof that storing a car like the 300SL too long can do more harm than good.

Says Kienle, "this is a car for driving," a fact to which most 300SL owners will attest.

Looks can be deceiving. These are not original 300SL Gullwing coupes, but nearly flawless reproductions designed and built by Tony Ostermeyer of Gullwing Cars in Gardena, California.

Authenticity and attention to details such as upholstery and luggage are Ostermeyer's trademarks. Many of the components he manufactures for his reproductions are good enough to use for a 300SL restoration. Windows, rubber seals, even latching and door mechanisms are perfect reproductions.

One feature that may make the Gullwing Cars reproduction 300SLs better than the originals is the addition of an air-conditioning system, which was not available back in the 1950s. Ostermeyer adds a Nardi steering wheel and more stylish shift boot. Gauges are reproductions and the car's engine, transmission, and suspension utilize current Mercedes-Benz components.

DESIGN CHANGES AND OPTIONS

Daimler-Benz AG built a total of 3,258 300SL cars from 1954 through 1962. This total production number breaks down into 1,400 coupes and 1,858 roadsters. Of the total production, 1,200 coupes and 1,458 roadsters are known to exist today. The majority of both models were originally sold in the United States and approximately 900 coupes and 1,100 roadsters remain here today. A great many cars have been returned to Germany, and there are probably more in the homeland today than when they were new. A fair number of 300SLs have also gone to Japan, Western Europe, and Great Britain.

Coupe Production Design Changes

Throughout the four-year production run of Gullwing coupes, a series of design changes were made, which began with the 1954 model year, chassis numbers 4500001 through 4500167.

Car 4500051 was the first to be equipped with a remote shift linkage, which did away with the ungainly long-neck 300 sedan shifter previously used. In its place was a short, chromed, straight-neck shifter fitted with a small engraved white plastic knob. Positioned along the center tunnel close to the driver's hand, it made faster and smoother shifts possible. Beginning with this same car, the clutch was also modified: the push rod actuated by the clutch pedal was replaced with a pull rod.

With car 4500152, the ZF steering was changed to DB steering, increasing the number of turns from lock-to-lock to reduce the car's oversteer condition which was aggravated by the swing axle rear suspension design.

While internal changes are not obvious unless the car is taken apart for restoration, external changes to the 300SL were numerous throughout the first year of production.

In the 1955 model year, cars 5500001 through 5500875, and beginning with car 5500075, the

bumper guards were altered from a more squared-off to a rounded-edge appearance more in keeping with the car's lines. The two most significant changes were to the grille and the fender "eyebrows," both of which were simplified for easier manufacturing. Beginning with 5500213 (the 379th coupe built), the welting placed between the fender and the "eyebrow" was eliminated and the brow was simply leaded into the fender. While this gave the "eyebrow" a more integrated appearance, it was nevertheless a significant change in the manufacturing of the car.

A change in the design and construction of the grille was the single most sweeping alteration to the appearance of the 300SL, although to the untrained eye it goes almost unnoticed. The early stars and the chromed barrels in which they were set in the center of the grille were concave, so that the star actually protruded beyond the circumference of the circle. The chromed wings inside the grille were also more gracefully curved. The process involved in manufacturing the original star required ten separate pieces: two for the star, seven for the barrel plus the back casting. This was simplified with the new star, which was constructed of just three pieces. These can be easily distinguished because the star and barrel are perfectly symmetrical. The new star and barrel were not as artistic as the original design, but far easier to manufacture.

A total of five mechanical alterations were made in 1955. The steering shock was changed beginning with 5500096. The drag link was changed beginning with 5500706. Improved brakes were added with 5500213. The treadle vac to an ATE brake system and the suspended accelerator pedal design was changed to a floor-mounted version with 5500752. The final alteration in 1955 was the removal of the electric pump grease fitting. Often forgotten, the upper bearing of the drive shaft of this pump is now greased by removing a plug.

The only interior modification for 1955 was confined to the ornamental dash bar, which was slightly changed.

The 1956 model year—cars 6500001 through 6500317—saw a second change to the ornamental dash bar and two major mechanical improvements. Beginning with 6500073 there was a pressure oil pump conversion. Instead of being driven directly off the crankshaft, where gear wear could cause loss of oil pressure but still allow continued engine operation, the pump was now operated in conjunction with the injection pump. Beginning with 6500150 a dual point/single coil ignition was used. This provided a 12 percent increase in dwell, which marked an important performance improvement.

Roadster Production Design Changes

The greatest number of running changes were made to the roadsters, which began with serial numbers 7500001 through 7500695 in 1957. The first models introduced leather upholstery, the racing cam and a 3.89:1 rear axle ratio as standard equipment. New features included a padded dash bar and the improved single-pivot swing axle rear suspension replacing the Gullwing's dual-pivot arrangement.

The most obvious interior changes between coupe and roadster were the relocation of the emergency brake handle from the driver's left to the right side of the seat and a completely revised dashboard layout with new instrumentation.

Beginning with 1958 models—8500001 through 8500350 and starting with 8500202—the seating surfaces were now completely perforated. Prior to this only the spaces between the pleats were perforated.

The most notable change to the 300SL roadsters began with the 1961 model year, 002701 through 003000. Starting with car 002780, four-wheel disc brakes became a standard feature.

In 1962—serial numbers 003001 through 003232 and beginning with 003049—roadsters were fitted with an aluminum block. A total of 209 alloy-block cars were built.

In the roadster's last full year of production, 1963—serial numbers 003233 through 003258—no modifications were made.

Horsepower Ratings

The 300SL Gullwing coupe was available with a number of options, the most important of which was the sports camshaft, which increased rated power from 215bhp DIN to 235bhp DIN. Interestingly enough, a 240bhp rating was most commonly the one given in advertising and in road tests conducted by automotive publications in 1954 and 1955. It is estimated that the sports camshaft was good for an increase of 20bhp. It was standard on the twenty-nine aluminum-alloy-bod-

ied coupes produced in 1955 and 1956 and on all 300SL roadsters.

There is often much confusion about the output of 300SL engines, and figures have varied from 215, 220, 235, and 240bhp for the coupes, to 235, 240, and 250bhp for the roadsters, all of which have been muddled about by DIN and SAE calculations. For the record, Daimler-Benz listed output for the 300SL coupe at 215bhp and for the roadster a figure of 235bhp. In the United States, 240bhp for the coupes and 250bhp for the roadsters have become the most commonly published figures. That notwithstanding, mathematically, 215 + 20 still adds up to 235 anyway you figure it.

Exterior and Interior Color and Trim

Perspective owners had quite a few choices to make when ordering their 300SL. The cars could be ordered from the factory with any available combination of paint, trim, and upholstery. However, Daimler-Benz had certain factory suggested color combinations for both coupe and roadster. The coupes were offered in

Location of the identification plates in the 300SL coupe as shown in the owners manual.

Daimler-Benz AG

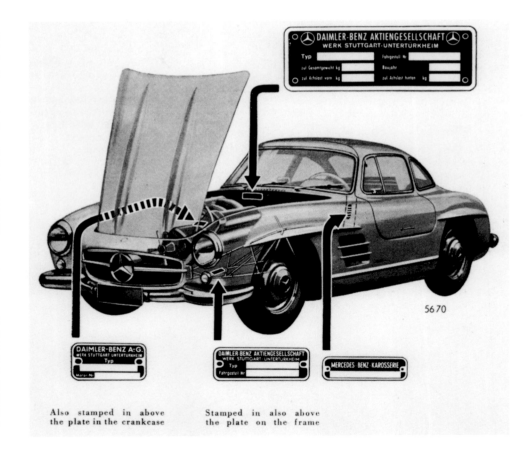

Also stamped in above the plate in the crankcase

Stamped in also above the plate on the frame

black, white, light gray, blue gray, silver gray, graphite gray (gunmetal), light blue, fire engine red, maroon, ivory, and strawberry red. Strawberry red was the most rarely see of all SL colors; only thirteen coupes were painted strawberry red.

Roadsters were available in black, white, light gray, blue gray, graphite gray (gunmetal), pearl green, light blue, fire engine red, and ivory. At least two roadsters were finished in strawberry red, although the color was not listed as being available after Gullwing production ended.

For roadsters fitted with the optional hardtop, colors available for the hardtop were black, white, light gray, graphite gray, and blue gray. Hardtops could also be special ordered to match any of the other exterior colors offered. The convertible top fabric was only available in black, tan, or dark blue.

There were, of course, special orders and at least one 300SL was finished in bright yellow, several in dark (British Racing) green, and a few roadsters were done in silver, although the color was not listed as being available.

Upholstery also varied from the standard list. Leathers were dyed in cream, natural, green, blue, black, red, and light gray. There were actually three different shades of red, two variations of blue and light gray respectively, and on strawberry cars upholstered in natural, the leather had slightly pink overtones to blend with the exterior color.

All roadsters came with leather upholstery, while coupes came standard with either blue, red, or green gaberdine plaid cloth and tex-leather upholstery. Leather was available as an option on the coupes.

Appendix 2
Specifications

300SL Coupe Specifications

Engine

Six-cylinder inline engine, one overhead camshaft driven by a duplex chain from the front end of the crankshaft, two valves per cylinder. The engine was available with two different camshafts: the standard camshaft had an outlet stroke of 0.31in, the sports camshaft with an outlet stroke of 0.33in, the inlet stroke being identical at 0.369in.

Maximum output	215bhp @ 5800rpm
Maximum torque	202lb-ft @ 4600rpm
Displacement	2992cc/3.0 ltrs/182.76ci
Bore	85mm/3.35in
Stroke	88mm/3.46in
Compression ratio	8.55:1
Optional US compression ratio	9.5:1

Fuel system	Bosch PES 6 KL 70/320 R 3 fuel injection
Lubrication	Dry sump

Transmission

All-synchromesh four-speed manual gearbox, cast-iron gearbox housing

Transmission ratios, 1st version (up to chassis number 40)

1st gear	3.14:1
2nd gear	1.85:1
3rd gear	1.31:1
4th gear	1.00:1
Reverse	2.57:1

Transmission ratios, 2nd version

1st gear	3.34:1
2nd gear	1.97:1
3rd gear	1.39:1
4th gear	1.00:1
Reverse	2.73:1
Standard final drive ratio	3.64:1
Optional final drive ratios	3.25:1, 3.42:1, 3.89:1, 4.11:1

(In addition to the final drive ratios specified, various other ratios were available for racing)

Top speed in gears by final drive ratio

	1st gear	2nd gear	3rd gear	4th gear
4.11:1	35mph	60mph	85mph	129mph
3.89:1	37mph	63mph	90mph	136mph
3.64:1	40mph	67mph	96mph	146mph
3.42:1	42mph	71mph	102mph	155mph
3.25:1	44mph	75mph	107mph	161mph

Chassis and Suspension

Double wishbones at the front with no-friction coil springs and rubber auxiliary springs. Hydraulic telescopic shock absorbers on all wheels. Front axle mounted to the frame by a transverse support arm. Torsion-bar anti-roll arm on front axle. Independent suspension at the rear by twin transverse control arms and coil springs reinforced by torsion bars fitted longitudinally on the frame.

There was also a special version with a stiffer suspension for customers participating in motorsports, fitted with harder springs and different shock valving.

Hydraulic drum brakes on all four wheels, duplex brakes at the front. Treadle-Vac brake servo up to chassis number 353, then replaced by ATE T 50 vacuum-type brake servo.

Recirculating-ball steering (except for the first 151 cars, which were fitted with ZF worm steering). Two revolutions of the steering wheel from lock-to-lock.

Standard tires	6.70x15 Continental or Engle bert front and rear
Optional tires	6.50x15 extra super-sport or 6.50x15 racing tires
Rim dimensions	5.50x15 J

Dimensions

Height	1300mm/51.2in
Width	1791mm/70.5in
Length	4521mm/178.0in
Wheelbase	2400mm/94.5in
Track, front	1384mm/54.5in
Track, rear	1435mm/56.5in
Fuel capacity	130 ltr/34.3 US gallons

300SL Roadster Specifications

Engine

Six-cylinder inline engine, one overhead camshaft driven by a duplex chain from the front end of the crankshaft, two valves per cylinder. The engine came standard with the sports camshaft with an outlet stroke of 0.33in and inlet stroke of 0.369in. There were minor differences between the coupe and roadster involving the fuel supply pump, the Bosch injection pump for engines with sports camshaft, and the injection nozzles.

Maximum output	235bhp @ 5800rpm
Maximum torque	202lb-ft @ 4600rpm
Displacement	2992cc/3.0 ltrs/182.76ci
Bore	85mm/3.35in
Stroke	88mm/3.46in
Compression ratio	8.55:1
Optional US compression ratio	9.5:1
Fuel system	Bosch PES 6 KL 70/320 R 3 fuel injection
Distributor	Bosch ZV/PCS 6 R 1 T
Coil	Bosch TK 12 A 10
Lubrication	Dry sump

Transmission

All-synchromesh four-speed manual gearbox, cast-iron gearbox housing
Transmission ratios

1st gear	3.34:1
2nd gear	1.97:1
3rd gear	1.39:1
4th gear	1.00:1
Reverse	2.73:1
Standard final drive ratio	3.64:1
Optional final drive ratios	3.25:1, 3.42:1, 3.89:1, 4.11:1

Chassis and Suspension

Double wishbones at the front with no-friction coil springs and rubber auxiliary springs. Hydraulic telescopic shock absorbers on all wheels. Front axle mounted to the frame by a transverse support arm. Torsion-bar anti-roll arm on front axle.

Single-joint swing axle at the rear with two coil springs and a third "compensation" coil spring intended to reduce swinging movements of the rear suspension.

Oil-pressure drum brakes on all four wheels, duplex brakes at the front. ATE T 50 vacuum-type brake servo.

Starting with chassis number 2780 in 1961, roadsters were fitted with Dunlop disc brakes on all four wheels.

Recirculating-ball steering. Two revolutions of the steering wheel from lock-to-lock.

Standard tires	6.70x15 touring special
Optional tires	6.70 - 15 extra super-sport
Rim dimensions	5.50x15 J

Dimensions

Height	1300mm/51.2in
Width	1791mm/70.5in
Length	4569mm/179.9in
Wheelbase	2400mm/94.5in
Track, front	1397mm/55.0in
Track, rear	1448mm/57.0in
Fuel capacity	100 ltr/26.4 US gallons

W196 S/Uhlenhaut 300SLR Coupe Specifcations

Engine

Eight-cylinder inline engine with power takeoff from the middle of the engine. Since the driveshaft came out of the middle of this straight-eight power unit, the M196 is actually two four-cylinder engines connected to each other. It features four overhead camshafts with forced operation of the two valves per cylinder (referred to as "Z" valve timing).

The crankshaft and connecting rods ran in roller bearings using the Hirth system. Mechanical Bosch fuel-injection system supplied fuel, which was ignited by Bosch double ignition. Dry sump lubrication was utilized with the oil tank placed to the left of the engine. The engine was installed in a horizontal arrangement at an angle of 33 degrees.

Maximum output	302bhp @ 7500rpm
Maximum torque	218lb-ft @ 5950rpm
Displacement	2992cc/3.0 Liters/182.51ci
Bore	78mm/3.07in
Stroke	78 mm/3.07in
Compression ratio	9.3.1

Transmission

Five-speed manual gearbox with synchromesh on

second through fifth gears. Various transmission ratios were fitted in accordance with specific requirements. The single-plate dry clutch measured 240mm/9.45in in diameter and was sprung by ten springs.

Chassis and Suspension

Independent suspension at the front on double wishbones (fastened to the wheel hub by ball joints). Independent suspension at the rear by twin transverse control arms with lowered point of rotation (Scheren-berg patent), double T-profile axle, wheels connected by welded tubes.

Drum brakes with fins (Al-fin) inside wheels, light-alloy cover outside for better air supply. Brakes measured 350mm/13.78in in diameter at the front; 275mm/10.83in at the rear. Twin-circuit brake system, hydraulic ATE brake servo increasing pedal pressure 2.6 times, hydraulic steering damper, hydraulic telescopic shock absorbers.

Tires, front	6.00x16
Tires, rear	7.00x16

Bodywork

Steel-tube spaceframe. Tubes measured 25mm/0.98in in diameter with a wall thickness of 1mm/0.04in. Magnesium body fitted directly onto chassis.

Dry weight	980.55kg/2,179lb
Weight in road trim	1106.55kg/2,459lb

Dimensions

Height	1300mm/51.18in
Width	1750mm/68.90in
Length	4400mm/173.23in
Wheelbase	2370mm/93.31in
Track, front	1330mm/52.36in
Track, rear	1380mm/54.33in
Fuel capacity	142 ltr/37.5 US gallons

Performance

Chassis number 0007/55 (license number W 216962) was made available to the Swiss motoring journal *Automobil-Revue* for testing in the summer of 1956. Performance measurements were as follows:

0–100km/h (62mph)	6.8 sec.
0–150 km/h (93mph)	13.6 sec.
0–200 km/h (124mph)	20.3 sec.
Top speed	290km/h/180.2 mph

Appendix 3
Production History

300SL Coupe

1954

Chassis Numbers	Production
First: 198 040-45 00001	166
Last: 198 040-45 00166	1954 Total: 166

1955

Chassis Numbers	Production
First: 198 040-55 00022	830
Last: 198 040-55 00877	
Aluminum-bodied cars:	26
198 040-55 00173	
198 043-55 00177	
198 043-55 00189	
198 043-55 00190	
198 043-55 00194	
198 043-55 00208	
198 043-55 00218	
198 043-55 00226	
198 043-55 00233	
198 043-55 00250	
198 043-55 00254	
198 043-55 00277	
198 043-55 00332	
198 043-55 00383	
198 043-55 00413	
198 043-55 00426	
198 043-55 00441	
198 043-55 00464	
198 043-55 00486	
198 043-55 00786	
198 043-55 00794	
198 043-55 00804	
198 043-55 00812	
198 043-55 00828	
198 043-55 00840	
198 043-55 00872	1955 Total: 856

1956

Chassis Numbers	Production
First: 198 040-65 00010	305
Last: 198 040-65 00317	
Aluminum-bodied cars	3
198 043-65 00015	
198 043-65 00023	
198 043-65 00033	1956 Total: 308

1957

Chassis Numbers	Production
First: 198 040-75 00007	70
Last: 198 040-75 00079	1957 Total: 70

300SL Roadster

1957

Chassis Numbers	Production
Out of series: 198 042-75 00037	3
198 042-75 00038	

198 042-75 00060
First: 198 042-75 00080 615
Last: 198 042-75 00694 1957 Total: 618

1958

Chassis Numbers	Production
First: 198 042-85 00065	267
Last: 198 042-85 00331	1958 Total: 267

1959

Chassis Numbers	Production
First: 198 042-95 00008	12
To: 198 042-95 00019	
From: 198 042-10-95 00020	89
To: 198 042-10-95 00108	
From: 198 042-10-002387	94
To: 198 042-10-002482	
198 042-10-002484	
198 042-10-002485	
198 042-10-002487	1959 Total: 200

1960

Chassis Numbers	Production
198 042-10-002483	
198 042-10-002486	
From: 198 042-10-002488	
To: 198 042-10-002715	
198 042-10-002717	
198 042-10-002719	
198 042-10-002721	
198 042-10002722	
198 042-10002723	
198 042-10002724	
198 042-10002727	
198 042-10002729	
198 042-10002730	
198 042-10002733	
198 042-10002734	1960 Total: 241

1961

Chassis Numbers	Production
198 042-10-002716	
198 042-10002718	
198 042-10002720	
198 042-10002725	
198 042-10002726	
198 042-10002728	
198 042-10002731	
198 042-10002732	
From: 198 042-10002735	
To: 198 042-10-002968	
From: 198 042-10-002970	
To: 198 042-10-002980	
From: 198 042-10-002983	
To: 198 042-10-002985	1961 Total: 256

1962

Chassis Numbers	Production
198 042-10-002969	
198 042-10002981	
198 042-10002982	
198 042-10002986	
198 042-10002987	
198 042-10002988	
From: 198 042-10002990	
To: 198 042-10-003129	
198 042-10-003131	
198 042-10003132	
198 042-10003133	
198 042-10003134	
198 042-10003135	
From: 198 042-10003137	
To: 198 042-10-003152	
198 042-10-003154	
From: 198 042-10-003157	
To: 198 042-10-003160	
From: 198 042-10-003162	
To: 198 042-10-003167	
198 042-10-003185	
198 042-10003213	
198 042-10003224	
198 042-10003225	1962 Total: 182

1963

Chassis Numbers	Production
198 042-10-003089	
198 042-10003130	
198 042-10003136	
198 042-10003153	
198 042-10003155	
198 042-10003156	
198 042-10003161	
From: 198 042-10003168	
To: 198 042-10-003184	
From: 198 042-10-003186	
To: 198 042-10-003206	
From: 198 042-10-003208	
To: 198 042-10-003212	
From: 198 042-10-003214	
To: 198 042-10-003223	
From: 198 042-10-003226	
To: 198 042-10-003229	
From: 198 042-10-003231	
To: 198 042-10-003256	
From: 198 042-10-003258	1963 Total: 91

1964

Chassis Numbers	Production
198 042-10-003207	
198 042-10003230	
198 042-10003257	1964 Total: 3

INDEX

Ascari, Alberto, 49

Bentley, W. O., 19
Bosch, 12
Bracco, Giovanni, 11, 34-35, 51
Braiq, Paul, 78
Brown, David, 19

Caracciola, Rudolf, 11, 33, 37-38
Chinetti, Luigi, 49, 75
Cleye, Rudy, 63-68
Collins, Peter, 138
Cunningham, Briggs, 75

Daetwyler, W. P., 36, 37
Daimler-Benz AG, 11-12, 60-61, 69, 129
Duncan, David Douglas, 98, 102-103

Engle, Werner, 68

Fangio, Juan Manuel, 21, 28, 136, 139-140
Ferrari, 11, 36, 46-47
Ferrari, Enzo, 19
Fitch, John, 50, 55, 68, 101, 138
Flock, Tim, 75

Geiger, Eugen, 50
Gendebien, Oliver, 68
Gross, Victor, 105
Grundfor, Scott, 100-119
Grupp, Erwin, 49, 50, 59

Helfrich, Theo, 41, 44, 101
Hermann, Hans, 136
Hill, Phil, 21

Hitzelberger, Edwin, 100, 102-103
Hoffman, Max, 12, 48, 60-61, 83, 97
Hoppe, Heinz, 60-61, 97

Jaguar, 11, 28-29, 137-138
Jenkinson, Denis, 138

Kiekhaefer, Carl, 75, 93
Kienle, Klaus, 61
Klenk, Hans, 41, 50, 52, 59
Kling, Karl, 11, 21, 33-35, 37-38, 41, 43, 50, 52, 59, 105, 136

Lang, Hermann, 33, 35, 38, 41, 43, 44, 46, 49, 50, 52, 59, 101, 136
Levegh, Pierre, 138
Lyons, Sir Williams, 19, 28-29

Macklin, Lance, 138
Mairesse, Willy, 69
McGriff, Hershel, 49
Mercedes-Benz models,
    300 sedan, 23-24
    C111, 31
    W125, 20-21
    W154, 21
    W163, 21
    W196, 129, 135
Mercedes-Benz 300SL models,
    aluminum-alloy Coupes, 69-71, 84-89
    Coupe, 53-61, 62-95
    preproduction Coupes, 34-35
    preproduction race cars, 33-61
    Roadster, 96-127
    SLR, 20, 128-145

SLS preproduction roadster, 22, 96-113
Metternich, Prince, 68-69, 83
Molter, Günter, 50
Moss, Stirling, 17, 28, 69, 138

Nallinger, Fritz, 19, 21, 22, 28, 33, 98-99, 100, 101, 102-103
Neubauer, Alfred, 19, 21, 22-27, 33-35, 39, 42-43, 50-52, 105, 136, 138
Niedermayer, Norbert, 41, 101
Nitske, Robert, 100-101

O'Shea, Paul, 63-68, 105, 107, 113

Parravano, Tony, 75
Porsche, 11, 45-46

Ricardo, Don, 75-78
Riess, Fritz, 36, 37-38, 41, 43, 44, 46

Sacco, Bruno, 30-31
Settember, Tony, 63

Tak, W. I., 68
Taruffi, Piero, 49

Uhlenhaut, Rudolf, 19-31, 43-44, 100, 105

Villoresi, Luigi, 49
von Neumann, John, 75

Wilfert, Karl, 19, 30, 52, 78, 98-99
Wilkins, Gordon, 139

Zampiero, Armando, 68